The Party
and the National Question in China

The Party

and the National Question in China

*George Moseley*

The M.I.T. Press

*Massachusetts Institute of Technology*
*Cambridge, Massachusetts, and London, England*

*To Eva*

This volume comprises a translation of a book by Chang Chih-i entitled, *A Discussion of the National Question in the Chinese Revolution and of Actual Nationalities Policy (Draft)*, to which have been added an introduction, notes, appendices, a bibliography, and an index.

While working on the present volume, the translator was a Research Fellow in the Department of Economic and Political Studies, School of Oriental and African Studies, University of London. He is particularly indebted to Mrs. Jacqueline Condron, then associated with the Department as a tutor in Chinese, for her assistance at many points in the original text.

# Contents

# Introduction

1. *About the author.*[1] A native of Wuhan, Chang Chih-i is a veteran Chinese Communist who had already made his mark in the Party by the time of the Marco Polo Bridge Incident in 1937. He was then serving as a political commissar to a brigade of the New Fourth Army. During the Sino-Japanese War he also ran the political bureau of a district in one of the Party's principal guerrilla areas, located on the Honan-Hupeh border. With the establishment of the Chinese People's Republic in 1949, Chang was put in charge of united-front activities and nationalities affairs for all of south-central China. This meant that, among other things, he

[1] (The translator's footnotes will be designated by superior numbers and the footnotes present in the original Chinese, by asterisks and daggers.) The author is not the Chang Chih-i who collaborated with Fei Hsiao-t'ung on *Earthbound China* (1945) nor the one who collaborated with Owen Lattimore and others on *Pivot of Asia* (1950). The Chang Chih-i whose book is translated here appears in *Gendai Chūgoku jinmei jiten* (Biographical dictionary of contemporary Chinese) (Tokyo, 1962), p. 370, and in U.S. Department of State, Bureau of Intelligence and Research, *Directory of Party and Government Officials of Communist China*, 2 vols. (Washington, 1960), Vol. 2, p. 5. The itemization of writings by Chang provided here is the result of my own research and is almost certainly incomplete. Chang is not an "intellectual," either of the Western or Chinese variety.

1

was responsible for dealing with the country's largest ethnic minority, the six million Chuang of Kwangsi Province, now the Kwangsi Chuang Autonomous Region.[2] In April 1955, a little over eighteen months before writing the book translated here, he became a Deputy Director of the United Front Work Department of the Chinese Communist Party (CCP). In 1957 he wrote a substantial article on "Several Questions Concerning the People's Democratic United Front,"[3] and in 1958 he produced a book-length treatment of the united front.[4] A fresh appraisal of the religious question among China's nationalities was written by Chang in 1962.[5]

As a department of the Central Committee, the United Front Work Department is the most direct link between the CCP leadership and the national minorities. In similar fashion, the Nationalities Affairs Commission of the State Council focuses central government policy on the national minorities, and the Nationalities Committee

[2] Chang's report on "The Present Situation and Future Prospects for Nationalities Work in the South Central Area," dated 30 December 1951, is among the *Collected Documents on Nationalities Policy* (Min-tsu cheng-ts'e wen-hsien wei-pien) published by the People's Publishing House, Peking, in 1953.

[3] "Kuan-yu jen-min min-chu t'ung-i chan-hsien ti chi-ko wen-t'i," *Hsin-hua pan-yüeh k'an* (New China semimonthly), No. 109 (1957, no. 11), pp. 67–71.

[4] *Shih-lun chung-kuo jen-min min-chu t'ung-i chan-hsien* (Peking, 1958).

[5] "Correctly Understand and Implement the Party's Policy on Freedom of Religious Belief," *Min-tsu t'uan-chieh* (Nationalities unity), No. 4 (April 1962), pp. 2–5. This article has been translated in U.S. Consulate General, Hong Kong, *Selections from China Mainland Magazines*, No. 318.

of the National People's Congress brings to the surface some reflection of opinion among the national minorities.[6] The groups with which the Department is specifically called upon to carry out its united front activities include, in addition to leaders of the national minorities, members of "democratic parties," religious leaders, non-Communist intellectuals, and so forth. Chang has also been prominent in the Chinese People's Political Consultative Conference (CPPCC), a public organization through which the CCP operates in its united-front work. Concurrently with his post in the United Front Work Department, Chang has been a deputy secretary-general of the CPPCC and a member of its Standing Committee. It is difficult to imagine a better vantage point from which to survey the national minority policy of the CCP than that actually occupied by Chang. So far as I am aware, he is the only important Chinese Communist to have attempted a systematic analysis of the CCP's theoretical approach to the national minority question. The importance of his work, then, should be obvious; nor has it diminished in the ten years since it was written.

The advantage of translating Chang's book, as opposed to paraphrasing it or simply using it as a source for my own analysis, is that much can be learned about the national minority question in China from the very way in which Chang treats it. This specific outlook could not but be distorted in any attempt to write *about* it; my own comments, aside from this Introduction, are limited to occasional footnotes. His attitude toward the

[6] See the organization chart provided in Appendix D.

national minorities, which reflects that of the Party, is partly that of a Han Chinese and partly that of a Communist, a synthesis of the two being the constant objective of the Chinese Communist Party with respect to the national question. The value of Chang's work is greatly heightened by the peculiar circumstances, described farther on in the Introduction, in which Chang is believed to have been writing at the end of 1956. *A Discussion of the National Question in the Chinese Revolution and of Actual Nationalities Policy (Draft)* is remarkably cogent and straightforward, and should therefore serve as a useful primer to the student of the national minority policy of the Chinese Communist Party, which represents a unique phase in the development of Marxism-Leninism and in the march of Chinese history.

2.  *The meaning of the terms "national question" and "nationalities work."* What is meant by "national question" in the title of Chang's book? It must be clarified if we are to fully appreciate Chang's analysis. It is important because, although it is highly theoretical in itself, policies developed in accordance with certain ideas about the national question vitally affect the lives of a great many people. As Chang himself says in the last chapter, Marxist-Leninist theory on the national question must be studied by Party members, for only thus can they equip themselves with the "ideological weapons" they need in order to carry out the Party's policy toward the national minorities. Marxist-Leninist theory on the national question defines a methodology

for dealing with specific questions concerning the status
of communities called nations or nationalities; therefore,
only Marxist-Leninist revolutionaries are confronted
with a "national question"; a "national question" cannot even arise unless there are Communists about (although there may, in their absence, be an "Irish question," a "Polish question," etc.). Party members are
carrying out "nationalities work" — another term which
is central to the present study — when they apply
Marxist-Leninist theory on the national question to
specific nationality problems.

According to Communists, the fundamental cleavages
of world society are along class rather than national
lines. "Nations" are artificial units which came into
being with the rise of capitalism and which are destined
to disappear when capitalism is replaced with Communism; nationalism is a club used by capitalists to
keep the world proletariat divided and subdued. When
the proletariat seizes power throughout the world, then,
according to the theory, nations and nationalism will
vanish. In practice, however, this problem has only
arisen, as it were, in reverse, in the case of revolutionary
movements in Austria-Hungary, Russia, and China —
that is, in multinational empires that threatened to break
up into national units if the revolution succeeded. How
was the "working class," as it seized power in these
states (of course, it never did in Austria-Hungary),
to overcome the national animosities that had developed
under the emperors and forge a new multinationalism
based on proletarian unity?

The theoretical elaborations made by the Austrian

Social Democrats in response to this question provided the base from which Lenin approached the national question in Russia; Lenin's and Stalin's work in this field provided the Chinese Communists, in their turn, with a point of departure in approaching the national question in China.[7] Not only does Chang acknowledge this debt, but, in order to justify the adoption by the Chinese Communist Party of a national minority policy different from that espoused by Lenin and Stalin, he seeks to show just how opportunistic the Bolshevik approach had been. This is one of the most interesting features of Chang's book, for he shows precisely how the national question has been used by the Communists in both countries to promote the attainment of revolutionary goals as interpreted by Great Russians and Han Chinese, respectively. And when one realizes that more than half the population of Russia at the time of the October Revolution consisted of peoples other than the Great Russians, and that more than half the territory of China "liberated" in 1949–1950 was inhabited by peoples other than Han Chinese, it will be appreciated how immensely important the national question was to the success of both revolutions. The national question has

[7] For the Austrian Social Democrats and Lenin, see Samad Shaheen, *The Communist (Bolshevik) Theory of National Self-Determination* (The Hague and Bandung, 1956), and Richard Pipes, *The Formation of the Soviet Union* (Cambridge, Massachusetts, 1957); there is no full, rigorous treatment of Soviet nationalities policy and the Chinese Communists, but useful discussions may be found in John DeFrancis, "National and Minority Policies," in *The Annals of the American Academy of Political and Social Science*, Vol. 277 (September 1951): *Report on China*, pp. 146–155, and G. F. Hudson, "The Nationalities of China," *St. Antony's Papers*, Vol. 7 (London, 1960), pp. 51–61.

been central, not peripheral, to the revolutions in both countries.

In concrete terms, what "Marxist-Leninist theory on the national question" as applied in Russia and China really means is that claims for national independence on the part of minorities in socialist countries is counter-revolutionary, and only in capitalist and colonial countries are such claims correct. Once the Communist Party, the vanguard of the proletariat, seizes power, then the oppression of one nationality by another is impossible; anyone still demanding independence, therefore, can only be an agent, witting or unwitting, of world imperialism and therefore an enemy of "the people." By similar arguments it is demonstrated that national minorities do not need their own Communist parties, since their interests are abundantly guaranteed by the unique Communist Party of the country. The Russians could not prevent the loss of Finland and Poland, nor the Chinese of Outer Mongolia (and Taiwan?); elsewhere it was the Red armies that assured the new socialist hegemony. With the national minority areas under effective military control, Communist Party cadres then took up the "ideological weapon" provided by Marxist-Leninist theory on the national question in order to win over the masses and the "patriotic" leaders of the national minorities. This is "nationalities work."

Thus far, this nationalities work has been a conspicuous success. Surely it is not entirely a matter of chance that the two great Communist powers of today are precisely those two empires which, as states, have not disintegrated, as have, all in this century, the Ottoman, Austro-Hungarian, and Western maritime empires. If national antagonisms contributed, as they obviously did, to the collapse of the old order in Russia and China — one the most backward of European countries and the other the sick man of Asia — then the success of the revolutions in the two countries must owe a great deal to the approach of the Soviet and Chinese Communist Parties to their nationality problems. Indeed, it may be said that in the Soviet Union, and possibly in China, too, the "national question," in the sense of a question concerning independent statehood for constituent nationalities, has been overcome. Problems of nationality relations remain, but these are not apt to involve serious claims to statehood. In effect, the actual status of the minority national groups in the two states has receded from that of "nations," once accorded them in theory, to "nationalities" or simply "national minorities."[8]

3. *Han Chinese expansionism.* The contradistinction between Han Chinese and national minorities repeatedly made by Chang suggests that the Han Chinese constitute a homogeneous, discreet community from whom the national minorities are readily distinguishable. In fact, however, the cultural gap between "Han Chinese" and

---

[8] It should be noted that the attitude of most Western governments toward minority groups is implicitly assimilationist (see Philip C. Jessup, "Self-Determination Today in Principle and in Practice," *Virginia Quarterly Review*, Vol. 33 [1957], pp. 174–188), and that national minorities as such have no status in international law. Yet nationality problems are endemic in the "new states" of Asia and Africa.

"minority" is often no greater than that between Han Chinese of different regions. There is an almost continuous ethnocultural spectrum extending from the northern, wheat-eating, Mandarin-speaking Chinese at one end to, at the other, the dark-skinned K'awa in the south who are primitive food-gatherers and speakers of a language of the Mon-Khmer family. In between are the more than 100 million "Han" Chinese of south-coastal China who speak dialects other than Mandarin and who, in fact, sometimes refer to themselves as *T'ang-jen* (men of T'ang, after the T'ang dynasty, seventh to tenth centuries) rather than as *Han-jen* (after the Han dynasty, third century B.C. to third century A.D.) and the more than ten million persons of the "national minorities" in south China who have been to varying extents acculturated to Chinese ways — to the point, in some cases, that they had no awareness of being different, of being a "minority," until they were informed of the fact by workers from the Chinese Academy of Sciences who came to their areas after 1949. The Chinese Communist lack of precision in differentiating national minority from Han Chinese is not only misleading in itself, but it tends to obscure the fact, recognized by earlier governments, that, essentially, China is composed of several important peoples, namely, the Chinese, the Mongols, the Tibetans, and the Turks of Sinkiang (in Chinese, *Han, Meng, Tsang, Hui*); the minorities of south China are as subsidiary to the dominant strain of Han Chinese as are the "T'ang" Chinese of south-coastal China.[9]

9 Under the Ch'ing dynasty (1644–1911), Manchuria, Mongolia, Sinkiang, and Tibet were administratively separate from "China proper,"

The question "Who are the Chinese?" is only just beginning to be asked by historians in Communist China. It is not a question that troubled the equanimity of traditional Chinese historians, convinced of their mission as the carriers of the world's highest civilization.[10] Psychologically, the Han Chinese only became a nation in response to Western imperialism; culturally, this movement was greatly reinforced by the literary reform movement led by Hu Shih and others. And nationalism has been a dominant feature of Chinese Communism. Yet much of China's heterogeneity — in speech, diet, and physical appearance — so often remarked upon by foreign visitors still remains.[11]

in which were included the minorities of south-central and southwest China as well as the south-coastal Chinese. Under the Republic established in 1911, a five-barred flag (later discarded by Chiang Kai-shek) was adopted to indicate the same four peoples plus the rapidly disappearing Manchus *(Man)*. And in practice the Communist regime recognized the same fact: an issue of banknotes circulated in 1955 was printed in four languages (appearing on the same banknote): Chinese, Mongol, Tibetan, and Uighur (the main Turkic group of Sinkiang). In other ways, too, these groups are given priority. For instance, in the listing of China's peoples given in the 1964 *Jen-min shou-ts'e* (People's handbook), the Mongols are followed by the Hui (Chinese Moslems), Tibetans, and Uighurs, an order that cannot be explained in any way except the status arbitrarily accorded them by the leadership.

[10] See Harold Kahn and Albert Feuerwerker, "The Ideology of Scholarship: China's New Historiography," *The China Quarterly*, No. 22 (April–June 1965), pp. 1–13.

[11] George B. Cressey has made this diversity remarkably clear in his *Asia's Lands and Peoples* (London, 1952). Marquis Ito, the Japanese statesman of the early twentieth century, once said that "China is one country in name, eighteen countries in fact" (referring only to the eighteen provinces of China proper). Cited in Joseph R. Levenson, *Liang Ch'i-ch'ao and the Mind of Modern China* (Cambridge, Massachusetts, 1953), p. 114. The local dialects continue to flourish: for an

With reference to its ethnic component, being "Chinese" is a dynamic quality. "Chineseness" may be likened to a geographical zone, a blurred place on the map, through which an unending stream of peoples has filtered in a north-south direction. Typically, the northern invaders were Turkic or Mongol, occasionally Tungusic, nomads. Without altogether displacing the existing population, they ever renewed the vitality of the Chinese as a race, and this clearly has much to do with the fact that China possesses the oldest continuous civilization known to mankind. As the "barbarians" from the north became Sinicized (i.e., civilized), the older strain of Chinese pushed further south, bringing Chinese culture to the barbarians whom they encountered.[12] *Pari passu*, the territory and population within the Chinese state and thus within the area of Chinese culture were expanding.

The empire of the Han dynasty, established on the basis of the unification of China achieved by the preceding Ch'in dynasty (221–206 B.C.), was already, it appears, a "multinational state," for one of the former feudal states incorporated in it, the state of Ch'u in the middle Yangtze valley, is thought to have been inhabited by a T'ai people. The regionalism of the "Han Chinese"

---

example of the Party's effort to popularize Mandarin in Shanghai, see Ch'en Lin-hu, "Let P'u-t'ung-hua Better Serve the Three Great Revolutionary Movements," *Kuang-min jih-pao*, 17 March 1965 (Survey of China Mainland Press), No. 3429.

12 The confrontation of the nomadic horseman with the settled life of the Chinese is the subject of Owen Lattimore's *Inner Asian Frontiers of China* (New York, 1940); Herold Wiens has studied the extension southward of the Chinese sociopolitical system in *China's March toward the Tropics* (Hamden, Connecticut, 1954).

is as old as this, too: for instance, the distinctiveness of the Szechuanese in the west can be traced to the state of Shu which had a quasi-independent existence prior to the Ch'in unification. Under the T'ang dynasty, as already noted, the Cantonese area in south-coastal China (whence the Vietnamese are thought to have migrated southward) was welded into the empire; and under the Ming (1368–1644), Yunnan and the southwest were effectively incorporated. On the whole, this southern movement was gradual and piecemeal, being characterized by an influx of Chinese colonizers from the north who mixed with the local people. The effects of commerce, war, further migration, and the operation of the imperial bureaucracy tended to knit these frontier areas more closely to the Chinese core area in the plain of the Yellow River without, however, obliterating their special characteristics.[13] The indigenous populations that have remained unabsorbed sometimes live side by side in discreet communities with the Chinese, sometimes retreat back into the hills, and sometimes attempt to emigrate southward. Thus, in any given national minority region of south China today there is a whole range of comparative "Chineseness" among the inhabitants which alto-

[13] An early stage of what may be the same process is to be observed in certain countries of Southeast Asia in modern times, where Chinese immigrants from certain localities (not Han Chinese in general) have mixed with the indigenous population. Overseas Chinese who have returned to the Mainland in recent years are often treated as if they were members of a national minority. Many have been settled in special areas set aside for them in Yunnan, Sinkiang, and other frontier regions; after resettlement, too, they have sometimes been treated as a group quite apart from the bulk of the Han Chinese.

gether eludes the dichotomy, "Han Chinese"–"national minority."

The Great Wall symbolizes the fact that for geographical reasons the Chinese were not able to expand to the north as they did to the south. This situation was modified with respect to Manchuria and Inner Mongolia by railroads built by Western enterprise that facilitated Chinese colonization. Thus, the Manchus disappeared and Manchuria became safely Chinese, dooming in advance the Japanese attempt to establish an independent "Manchukuo." And Inner Mongolia had become overwhelmingly Chinese by the time the Inner Mongolia Autonomous Region was created in 1947. On the other hand, Outer Mongolia, Sinkiang, and Tibet retained their uniqueness: although held by successive Chinese dynasties, the imperial administration was always unstable because it lacked the ballast of a sizable Han Chinese community. They were tied to China without ever becoming Chinese. Outer Mongolia broke away altogether and succeeded in establishing an independent state. Tibet might have done likewise had foreign influence there developed to the point, as it did in Outer Mongolia, of creating a secular leadership with a national perspective. Only the indifference, apathy, or complicity of the Soviet Union can explain China's retention of Sinkiang, her "wild west," as Lattimore once called it. With the modern transportation and communication facilities developed by the Chinese Communists, the colonization of Sinkiang and Tibet is now proceeding, although it has encountered bitter resistance.

Meanwhile, the Mongolian People's Republic, recognized by China, continues to go its own way. Had Outer Mongolia not broken away, its people today would merely count as one of China's "national minorities," as is the case with the people of Tibet and the Uighurs and Kazakhs of Sinkiang. To juxtapose the people of Outer Mongolia with various unhistorical, scattered, half-assimilated ethnic groups of south China is to demonstrate how far from a reflection of the objective situation is the distinction between Han Chinese and national minority. This lack of proportion is revealed in more concrete terms by the fact that, while the Han population in Sinkiang and Tibet was nil, in 1949 Han Chinese comprised more than half of the total population of all China's national minority areas averaged together.

What the distinction between Han Chinese and national minority does reflect is a traditional Chinese attitude toward China's frontier peoples as occupants of a zone midway between the Han Chinese center and the regions of outer barbarians, or foreigners, with the tributary states (much of East and Southeast Asia) occupying a special position. The primary distinction between the Han Chinese and China's frontier peoples was that the latter did not, in general, use the Chinese system of writing, the principal ingredient of "Chinese" culture and the cement which held together a people who often spoke mutually unintelligible dialects. This situation has presented the Chinese Communists with a dilemma that remains unresolved: in the interests of China's multinational unity, the adoption of a phonetic script for

the whole country was desirable, but the abandonment
of the Chinese characters would adversely affect the
unity of the Han Chinese who, after all, comprise the
core group of the nation.

4. *The "creative application" of Marxist-Leninist theory on the national question to the concrete conditions of the Chinese revolution.*   While a certain amount of
intellectual chicanery was involved in wedding the two,
there was a high degree of compatibility between the
traditional Chinese attitude toward China's non-Han
peoples and Marxist-Leninist theory on the national
question. For "non-Han" could be substituted "feudal"
or "prefeudal," while for "Han" could be substituted
"capitalist" or "modern." At the time of Liberation, so
the argument goes, only the Han people (plus, it is con-
ceded, "a very few" — never specified — national minorities) had emerged as a modern nation, with a mode
of production characteristic of the capitalist era. With
the liberation of all the peoples of China, therefore, it
became a sacred duty of the Han "proletariat" to render
assistance to the "laboring masses" of the national minorities in order that they might rapidly emerge from
their backwardness. Since Han assistance was the best
guarantee of the development of the national minorities,
any demand on their part for separation from China
would, by definition, be contrary to the interests of
their own laboring masses and therefore wrong.

This approach served the practical requirement of
masking the real differences that existed among the
"national minorities" and of isolating them as a group.

What the national minorities had in common was a profound distrust for the Han people and an almost complete lack of revolutionary enthusiasm. To have failed to discriminate between them and the Han Chinese would have been to overlook the real danger of the revolution bogging down on account of non-Han resistance. Regional autonomy, the result of the creative application of Marxist-Leninist theory to the national question in China, made it possible for the Han Chinese revolution to proceed while the non-Han revolution lagged behind, as the Chinese Communist leadership knew that it inevitably would. In effect, it divided the Chinese revolution into two stages, although in fact the second, or non-Han stage, has been subdivided into almost as many steps as there were national minorities (with the Tibetans at the end of the line).

A national minority which is not ready for the socialist "transformation" of its society, as the Han people are, must necessarily, according to Communist theory, lack a developed working class, but if this is the case then how can the nationality make any choice about its association with the Han Chinese in the Chinese People's Republic? This is a fundamental contradiction in the national minority policy of the CCP. Within the framework of the policy itself only a time gap can be admitted in lieu of this contradiction. And this time gap is the opportunity for the Party to perform its "nationalities work," which means to destroy the inherent unity of the national minority and to introduce class divisions in its place. Meanwhile, the "autonomous area" within which the national minority finds itself serves to contain resistance or rebellion while the operation is being performed. "Regional autonomy" is the opposite of what its name implies: "regional detention" would be more descriptive.

As Chang Chih-i himself observes, there is a close connection between the national question and the religious question in China, in that the non-Han peoples are comparatively religious; moreover, their religious unity and their national unity overlap. The CCP is determined to efface both characteristics, replacing them with a proletarian outlook. The methods to be employed in each instance are similar. Cadres are called upon to take a charitable attitude toward the "laboring masses" who have, through no fault of their own, been duped by their religious and national leaders. By means of united-front tactics, the latter are to be encouraged to contribute to the development of their people and to participate in patriotic activities, such as mass campaigns and the like. The Party has recognized, as Chang indicates, that many of these leaders retain considerable influence among their peoples and that the Party's "nationalities work" will suffer if they are not won over to the support of the Party's program of reform and development for the nationality. Simultaneously, at the mass level, the Party is to recruit Communist Party and Government cadres whose favorable attitude toward the CCP is presumed to have been assured by new measures taken in the interest of social reform and economic development.

Events showed that, so long as Han Chinese interests remained paramount, the Party could have unity without reform, or reform without unity, but not both at the same time. It had the first during the period 1949 to 1956 and the second from 1956 to 1962. Since 1962 a new policy seems to have emerged.[14] So close is the new policy, in its essence, to the recommendations proferred by Chang that it would almost seem as if members of the Central Committee had just got around to reading his book. Events have forced the Party to retreat to the more moderate approach long urged by those most intimately connected with national minority work, who had warned against the use of strong-arm methods in attaining revolutionary objectives in the frontier regions of the country. Writing in 1956, at a time when the Party's national minority policy was under intensive review, Chang was not able to determine the course which the Party's policy was then to take, but in the years that followed the fallacy of the line actually adopted became plain for all to see.

A striking feature of the Party's new approach is that it takes account of the fact that the national minorities are so many distinct entities and not simply a collectivity of non-Han peoples. The traditional Han Chinese attitude toward the frontier peoples, with which Marxist-Leninist policy on the national question was found to be compatible, an attitude in which the non-Han peoples were held to be at a lower stage of civilization as compared with the Han, has broken down. In the Party's new attitude, the national minorities can be discerned

[14] See the author's "China's Fresh Approach to the National Minority Question," *The China Quarterly*, No. 24 (September–December 1965), pp. 15–27.

individually: out of the creative application of Marxist-Leninist theory on the national question to the concrete conditions of the Chinese revolution a new synthesis has thus emerged.

5. *The 1956 focus.*  So far as can be ascertained from his published writings, the national minority question is not an aspect of China's affairs that has especially interested Mao Tse-tung. He has dealt with particular national minority problems when such have become serious enough to threaten the fortunes of the CCP or, since Liberation, to perturb the national scene, but he is not known to have favored any specific "line" on the national question in China. This lacuna is made only more noticeable by Chang Chih-i's effort in Chapter Two to substantiate a claim for an important "Maoist" contribution to Marxist-Leninist theory on the national question. In sum, Mao's is a typically Han-Chinese approach to the matter. The corollary of his lack of concern about the national minorities as such is his very deep concern about the adhesion to China of the vast territories inhabited by them. For Mao, the inhabitants were but one of the given characteristics of the frontier regions, and one that was not unalterable.

Theoretical analyses of China's national minority question flourished during two periods. The first was during the CCP's development prior to 1935, the year that marked Mao's ascension to power within the CCP leadership and the shift to the hinterland of the locus of the Chinese revolution. During this period the ques-

tion received highly rudimentary and abstract treatment.[15] The second period extended from the "liberation" of the national minority areas, completed by the
end of 1952, until the transitional stage 1956 to 1958.
This second period corresponded to the accentuated
policy of "leaning to one side," that is, of reliance on
the Soviet Union.

The CCP had seized power throughout the country
by relying on the People's Liberation Army and the
slogans of the united front, which it had not ceased to
employ since the mid-thirties.[16] In exchange for the
promise of complete national equality and the right to
manage their own affairs once the revolution was victorious, China's non-Han peoples were called upon to
unite with the Han in opposing imperialism. This anti-
imperialist united front carried the CCP through the
stage of "democratic reform" during which a certain
amount of land distribution was carried out and the
most notorious "reactionaries" and Kuomintang col-
laborators were disposed of, but by the summer of 1956,
with the collectivization movement sweeping China, its
usefulness had been exhausted.

Between 1952 and 1956 many Soviet experts had
come to China for the purpose of helping workers from
the Nationalities Institute of the Chinese Academy of
Sciences to identify the various national groups in China
and classify their languages. This was preliminary to
the implementation of regional autonomy, promised

[15] The most elaborate CCP statement of the time is reproduced in
Appendix B.
[16] Good examples of the latter are provided by Chang in Chapter Two.

in the Common Program of 1949.[17] In 1954 the Nationalities Institute began to publish a journal, called *Min-tsu wen-t'i i-tsung* (Translations on nationalities problems), which consisted of translations of Russian and East European material, or of contributions from Russian specialists, on national minority affairs, and a number of complimentary treatments of China's handling of nationality problems appeared in the Soviet Union.[18] At the same time, the Nationalities Institute itself was under the influence of a group of sociologists led by the Western-trained Fei Hsiao-t'ung and Lin Yüeh-hua who sought to persuade the CCP leadership that in the movement of the whole country toward socialism, socialism for the national minorities ought to be grafted to the individual societal structure in each case.[19] Chang Chih-i lays this matter to rest in Chapter One.

[17] See Appendix C. The Common Program, dated 29 September 1949, was drawn up prior to the arrival of the PLA in the important frontier regions (exclusive of Inner Mongolia and Manchuria).

[18] For instance, A. G. Yakovlev, "Economic Construction in the Nationality Regions of the Chinese People's Republic," *Voprosy Ekonomiki*, No. 1 (1955), pp. 122–130, and B. F. Kasatkin, "Solution of the National Question in the Chinese People's Republic," *Sovetskoye Vostokovedeniye*, No. 4 (1956), pp. 16–27. A sharp attack from Taiwan on CCP nationalities policy was directed in part at this Soviet influence: Chang Hsia-min, *Kung-fei pao-cheng hsia chih pien-chiang min-tsu* (The border peoples under the tyranny of the Communist bandits) (Taipei, 1958).

[19] Their position was put forward in a series of three articles which they wrote jointly for *Jen-min jih-pao* (10, 14, and 16 August 1956) and which have been translated in U.S. Consulate General, Hong Kong, *Current Background*, No. 430; it was stated rather more directly in a report delivered by Lin in May 1956 at an ethnography conference held in Leningrad (see Lin Yüeh-hua, "Problems Confronting Chinese Ethnographers in Connection with Solving the Nationalities Question in the Chinese People's Republic," *Sovetskaya Etnografiya*, No. 3 (1956), pp.

The Twentieth Congress of the Soviet Communist
Party, at which "de-Stalinization" was inaugurated, and
the speed-up in the tempo of China's "socialist transformation," both coming in 1956, created deep uneasi-
ness among all those concerned with nationalities work
in China. On the one hand, the position of the Soviet
advisers was threatened (they were all withdrawn a few
years later); on the other, the sociologists began to feel
the pressure of the Party professionals. During the summer of 1956, both the Soviet and Chinese groups, fearful lest their work be overtaken by "socialist transformation," were busily engaged in a sociological
survey among the national minorities. There was un-
easiness in the frontier regions, too, where the cooperative movement had been launched among China's
non-Han peoples, some of whom knew of the Hungarian
revolt.[20] The attempt to pool privately owned livestock
had created a tense situation in Inner Mongolia, while
armed resistance — the prelude to the great Tibetan
revolt of 1959 — had flared up among the Tibetan
herders of Szechwan Province.

---

79–91, translated in Joint Publications Research Service, No. 16,431
[30 November 1962], pp. 1–32).

Fei edited a collection of papers apparently written by associates in
the Nationalities Institute and published in Hong Kong in 1956 under
the title *Shen-ma shih min-tsu ch'ü-yü tzu-chih* (What is national
regional autonomy?). The first piece, with the same title as the book,
was written by Fei. The other pieces deal with various autonomous
areas. The whole is on a popular level.

[20] In an unpublished paper entitled "Traditional Tibet: The First
Ten Years of Effort at Integrating Tibet into the People's Republic of
China," Edward Friedman has suggested that the change in China's
attitude toward the Hungarian revolt, from one of sympathy to one of
condemnation, sprang from her concern over her own frontier regions.

Such was the atmosphere in which Chang Chih-i was writing at the end of 1956. *A Discussion of the National Question in the Chinese Revolution and of Actual Nationalities Policy (Draft)* appears to have been written hastily as a position paper to provide a basis for discussion within the Party on nationalities policy. Its straightforward, cryptic style sets it apart from the general run of more or less propagandistic material about nationalities problems which has appeared in the CPR. Its publication as a book is unusual, too. The views of important CCP personalities on questions of policy customarily appear in one of the Party's theoretical journals. Probably an article would not have provided sufficient space for the extensive analysis required, and a book had the further advantage that it could be printed and distributed immediately to those for whom it was intended.[21]

In the summer of 1957, scarcely six months after the appearance of Chang's book, a new policy line was set by a nationalities work conference held at the coastal city of Tsingtao. Whether Chang's thesis was overtaken by events or whether it simply failed to impress the Party leadership we do not know: in any case, there was little trace of Chang's recommendations to be found in the line adopted by the conference, which was laid down in a report by Premier Chou En-lai.[22] The conference

[21] Although I have no special knowledge about the book's distribution, it seems unlikely that it was widely disseminated. The copy from which the present translation was made is the property of the Library of the Harvard-Yenching Institute, Cambridge, Massachusetts. There are also copies in the Library of Congress and at the School of Oriental and African Studies, London.

[22] See *Jen-min Jih-pao* (24 August 1957). Also, U.S. Consulate General, Hong Kong, *Survey of China Mainland Press*, No. 1605).

singled out local nationalism rather than big Han chauvinism as the principal obstacle to the successful implementation of the CCP's nationalities policy, whereas Chang had devoted the final chapter of his book to the opposite view. In general, the aim of the new line was to crush opposition on the part of the national minorities to the socialist reforms deemed necessary by the CCP, whereas Chang had urged a more cautious approach.

It can be seen that Chang was writing in what might be described as a policy "trough," between Mao's call for collectivization (summer 1955) and the tough policy subsequently adopted in order to achieve it: at the end of 1956 a reaction on the part of the national minorities against the new policy of collectivization could be observed, but a policy specifically designed to cope with this reaction was not to emerge until the following spring.[23] Chang also stands midway between the "soft" line of the sociologists and the "hard" line of the regular Party men. As an important CCP member himself, he is one who has made national minority affairs his specialty: his special knowledge and experience in this area thrust upon him the responsibility of advising the Party leadership with respect to national minority affairs, but the leadership may not have desired, or may not have been able, to adopt the line that conformed best to the

[23] In fact, nationalities policy has enjoyed little real autonomy: in general, shifts in policy with regard to the national minorities run parallel to shifts in policy regarding national affairs in general. This was especially noticeable in 1957–1958, when the antirightist campaign among the Han people took the form of an antilocal nationalist campaign vis-à-vis the national minorities.

CCP's long-range interests as interpreted by its own expert.[24]

It is undoubtedly because things were so much in flux at the time he was writing that Chang's book is so revealing. And it is for this reason that it remains important today, for such a free atmosphere has not occurred again. In the summer of 1957 Fei Hsiao-t'ung was denounced,[25] and at the end of 1959 *Min-tsu yen-chiu* (Nationalities research), the scholarly journal that had taken the place of *Min-tsu wen-t'i i-tsung* (Translations on nationalities problems) only a year earlier, was suppressed in its turn, being superseded by *Min-tsu t'uan-chieh* (Nationalities unity), a journal that, being uncorrupted by "bourgeois science," could better reflect the Party's new line.[26] After several years of repression

[24] In the jargon of the Party, Chang was neither all "red" nor all "expert" but rather "red and expert" — the ideal.

[25] Fei Hsiao-t'ung, "I Admit My Guilt to the People," speech delivered to the fourth session of the First National People's Congress, 13 July 1957, and published in *Jen-min jih-pao* (14 July 1957) (U.S. Consulate General, Hong Kong, *Current Background*, No. 470); Lin Yüeh-hua, "The Treacherous and Ugly Fei Hsiao-t'ung," *Jen-min jih-pao* (2 August 1957) (*Current Background*, No. 475); and (Mrs.) Elsie Hawtin, "The 'Hundred Flowers Movement' and the Role of the Intellectual in China. Fei Hsiao-t'ung: A Case History," *Papers on China* (Harvard University, Center for East Asian Studies), Vol. 12 (December 1958), pp. 147–198.

[26] Maurice Friedman has reviewed the demise of the social sciences in his article, "Sociology in and of China," *British Journal of Sociology*, Vol. 13 (1962), pp. 106–116. For Chinese Communist criticism of "bourgeois" anthropology and sociology, see the article by Hsieh Fu-min entitled "Liang-nien lai shao-shu min-tsu she-hui li-shih tiao-ch'a kung-tso ti chi-pen tsung-chieh" (Basic summing up of the past two years' investigation work into the social history of the national minorities), which appeared in the first issue of *Min-tsu yen-chiu* (Nationalities research) (pp. 2–12) when it began publication in 1958. Hsieh's article, originally

(1958 to 1960, also the years of the Great Leap Forward), a new policy made its appearance in 1962. This policy accords remarkably well with the ideas presented by Chang which, there seems little doubt, still remain an excellent guide to the study of the national question in China.

---

presented as a speech to a "great leap forward" conference on national minority investigation work, attacks the "Fei Hsiao-t'ung rightists" in particular.

# Chang Chih-i

*Chung-kuo ko-ming ti min-tsu wen-t'i ho min-tsu cheng-ts'e chiang-hua (t'i-kang)*
[A Discussion of the National Question in the Chinese Revolution and of Actual Nationalities Policy (Draft)]

(Peking: China Youth Publishing House, 1956), 76 pages.

# CHAPTER ONE

# Our Country Is a United, Multinational State

*The Chinese People's Republic is a state in which many nationalities are united.* Within the large family of our vast motherland, besides the Han people who make up more than 90 per cent of the population of the whole country, there are also people of the Mongol, Hui, Tibetan, Uighur, Miao, Yi, Chuang, Pu-yi, Korean, Manchu, Kazakh, T'ung, Pai (Min-chia), T'ai, K'awa, Ha-ni, Yao, Li, T'u-chia, Tung-hsiang, Kirghiz, T'u, Li-su, Nung, Na-hsi, La-hu, Shui-chia, Ching-p'o, Ch'iang, Kao-shan, Tatar, Russian, Uzbek, Tajik, Pao-an, Yu-ku, Salar, Sibo, Olunch'un, and several tens of other nationalities. The population of the national minorities amounts to more than thirty-five million in the whole country, representing 6.06 per cent of the national population (not including overseas Chinese, students abroad, and the still unliberated population of Taiwan). Among them, there are ten minorities with populations of more than a million, as follows: Mongol, 1,460,000; Hui, 3,500,000; Tibetan, 2,770,000; Uighur, 3,640,000; Miao, 2,510,000; Yi, 3,250,000; Chuang, 6,610,000; Pu-yi, 1,240,000; Korean, 1,120,000; and Manchu, 2,410,000. Among the other minorities, all of which

29

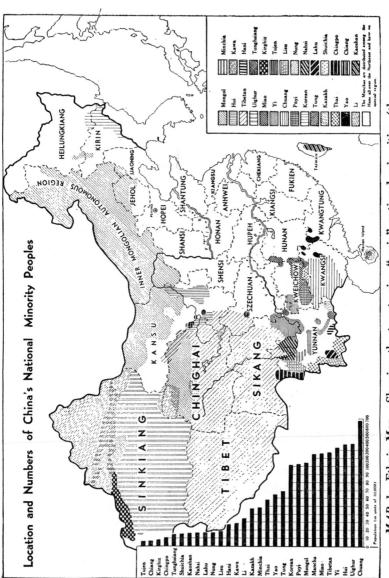

MAP 1: Ethnic Map. Showing the twenty-nine "main" national minorities (those represented in the National People's Congress as of March 1955).*

* From *China Reconstructs* (March 1955), p. 10. The orthography of this map varies slightly from that used in Appendix A and the text.

have populations of less than a million, the smallest is the Olunch'un with only a little over 2,200 people.[1]

*China's national minorities are found in all parts of the country, but they are concentrated in the border regions.* The Mongols dwell together in the Inner Mongolia Autonomous Region and in northeastern Heilungchiang Province; in Jehol and northwestern Kansu Provinces; and in Sinkiang, Tsinghai, and other provinces. The major Hui concentrations are in Kansu, Tsinghai, and other provinces of the northeast, but they are also found in other parts of the country, living in small communities of their own or dispersed among other peoples. The Tibetans live together in Tibet, Szechwan, Tsinghai, Kansu, and other provinces. The Uighurs, Kazakhs, Kirghiz, and some other peoples are concentrated in Sinkiang. The Chuang dwell together in Kwangsi. The T'ai, Ching-p'o, K'awa, Li-su, and others live in the frontier regions of Yunnan Province. The Yi are found in Szechwan, Yunnan, Kweichow, and other provinces. The Miao live principally in the three provinces of Hunan, Kweichow, and Kwangsi. The Koreans reside in the Yen-pien region of Kirin Province. The Yao live chiefly in the contiguous areas of Kwangsi, Kwangtung, and Hunan. The Li dwell together on the Island of Hainan in Kwangtung Province. The T'u-chia live in the northwestern region of Hunan Province. The Kaoshan are found on Taiwan. The other national mi-

---

[1] See Appendix A for a composite list of China's national minorities. Chang's population figures are taken from the 1953 census, whereas those in Appendix A are from an estimate for 1957. Map 1 shows their distribution.

norities are distributed principally in Heilungchiang, Liaoning, Kirin, Sinkiang, Tsinghai, Kansu, Szechwan, Yunnan, Kweichow, Kwangtung, Kwangsi, and other provinces, as well as in the Inner Mongolia Autonomous Region. The area inhabited by the various national minorities represents approximately 60 per cent of the total area of the whole country: in other words, their numbers are small, but their terrain is vast.

*The national minority areas of our country contain extremely rich natural resources.* These areas possess fabulous wealth in the form of coal, iron, petroleum, and nonferrous and other rare metals. China's chief livestock-producing areas, representing two-fifths of the total area of the country, are in the national minority areas; the forest reserves in the national minority areas are also exceptionally rich, amounting to one-sixth of the country's total forested area. All of these natural resources provide favorable conditions for the work of socialist construction in the whole country and are an important material foundation for our country's progress in building large-scale undertakings.

We often say that China is "large, naturally rich, and populous," but it is the national minority regions within our frontiers that possess the two characteristics of large size and natural wealth. And as for particular national minorities in particular localities, moreover, their populations may constitute a majority of the population, and this absolute majority may be quite large. When we call them national minorities, therefore, it is only in the context of the country as a whole and in comparison with the more than 560,000,000 people of the Han nationality.

*Like the Han, each of the national minorities in our country is dauntless, hard-working, frugal, determined, and good; each has contributed in different ways to the formation of our great motherland; and all of them together constitute the great family of the motherland — the indivisible People's Republic of China of which each of them is an integral part.*

The national minorities of our country depend mainly upon farming, herding, and logging for their livelihood. National minority groups with an aggregate population of approximately 30,000,000 are engaged in agriculture, 3,000,000 in herding, and 1,000,000 in the exploitation of the forests.

There are great differences among the national minorities of our country with regard to their respective stages of socioeconomic development. In areas inhabited by some thirty million of the total national minority population of thirty-five million, the socioeconomic structure is identical with, or very similar to, that in the Han regions of the country, while in the areas inhabited by the other five million members of national minorities, the situation is basically dissimilar or completely different as compared with the Han regions. Among the latter, not only is the feudal system retained by some groups, but the slave system, even more backward than feudalism, survives among some others. Before Liberation, some of them still retained important survivals of the mode of production characteristic of late primitive society. Since the investigations and research of the organizations concerned are insufficient and our data incomplete, we are still unable to make any final judgments concerning the historical stage occupied by certain nationalities. If our material were complete, our studies of Chinese history and of historical materialism would be greatly aided. It is, especially, material for a history of social evolution which is required. Such data could be compiled on the basis of the living evidence on China's nationalities and would be found to follow a clear pattern. It would then no longer be necessary for us to "constantly refer to Greece and Rome."[2] According to the analysis of social science, nationalities that do not, on the basis of their stage of development, constitute modern nations, are tribes, while some still remain within a more primitive lineage system. Even though we cannot, because our practical investigation work remains inadequate, take them up one by one for analysis and classification, there is no need to distinguish between tribes and lineages in actual administrative matters. Politically, all these problems must definitely be dealt with as nationality problems. Fundamentally, Stalin's four criteria for defining a nation[3] provide a

[2] In sociological writings available in China, reference was often made to Greece and Rome in descriptions of slave society, while Henry Lewis Morgan's investigations of American Indian life were widely cited in descriptions of primitive society.

[3] Stalin's four criteria, enunciated in 1912, are language, territory, economic life, and psychological makeup. A nation, he said, is "a historically constituted, stable community of people, formed on the basis of a common language, territory, economic life, and psychological makeup manifested in a common culture." J. Stalin, *Marxism and the National and Colonial Question* (London: Lawrence and Wishart, 1947), p. 8.

basis for the task of distinguishing among nationalities. As Marxist-Leninists we must naturally base our understanding on Marxist-Leninist principles. It is recognized in Marxism-Leninism that "nations are historically determined . . . , having been formed at the time of the collapse of feudalism and the rise of capitalism." We endorse this thesis. But it refers only to present-day nations, to nations of the capitalist period. This scientific theory is applicable to only those nationalities of China, in addition to the Han, that can be considered nations of the modern period: there are only a few main nations; the rest can only be thought of as tribal peoples in a premodern stage. Similarly, the Han were a tribal people during a long period prior to their emergence as a modern nation. The question of the date of the formation of the Han people as a modern nation has still not been answered by contemporary scholarship; however, one point must be clearly accepted, namely, that the emergence of the Han as a nation, in the modern sense of the term, must have occurred during China's feudal period,[4] when the mode of production characteristic of capitalism was beginning to appear. Another point can be accepted: before becoming a modern nation, the Han people comprised a unit that had a very long existence in Chinese history. Just as a number of kinship groups can develop together into a modern nation, so one kinship system can form several nations; it also happens

---

[4] Chinese Communist scholars have not arrived at a final periodization, following Marxist theory, of Chinese history: "China's feudal period" only means sometime prior to the Opium War. See Albert Feuerwerker, "China's History in Marxian Dress," *American Historical Review*, Vol. 66, No. 2 (January 1961), pp. 323–353.

that a single kinship group emerges as a single nation. As for the Han, they developed from a single kinship system into one modern nation. In dealing with the national question in China, therefore, we cannot dogmatically apply Stalin's theory which states that only when all four characteristics are present can a group be defined as a nation. This is because those peoples of China, comparatively small in number, who are dissimilar from the Han, have for a long time been uniformly regarded as national minorities, and the inequality of their status has increased as a result of oppression and discrimination. Therefore, this must be dealt with according to the policy of national equality. Regardless of how a particular nationality appears to stand in relation to kinship-group or tribal modes of organization, with respect either to its present or past situation, we must all positively and gradually guide it in the transition to socialism, helping these peoples to complete their development into socialist nations. It is therefore mandatory that we have the same policy for each nationality. Whenever these comparatively small peoples mingled with a larger nation, and especially the Han, there was danger of their being absorbed or even forcibly assimilated.

Reciprocal amalgamation between nationalities, on the other hand, is an existing phenomenon. The more that different nationalities come into contact, the more they influence one another, especially when one of the nationalities is comparatively advanced in government, economy, and culture and therefore in a position to influence heavily the more backward nationality. Over a long period of time, this mutual influence will naturally produce a new psychological identification that will lead to the gradual disappearance of the original differences between them. This kind of natural assimilation is an unavoidable and progressive phenomenon as well as a natural law. We are opposed, however, to an assimilationist policy. The more a policy of oppression and assimilation is employed, the more fearful are the minority nationalities of losing their identity and the more a spirit of fierce resistance is produced among them; only by letting them base the development of their political, economic, and cultural life on their own special characteristics can the ways of life of each of the nationalities be brought closer together and improved; in this way, they can more easily be induced to cast off their backwardness. This is appropriately dialectical.

Owing to China's long "stagnation" in a feudal economic system, it was the imperialists, whose big guns broke open the gates of antiquated China from the time of the Opium War, who brought about the awakening of all of China's nationalities. But the nationalities thereupon became subservient to the combined force of imperialism and domestic feudalism, making it impossible for domestic capitalism to develop successfully and causing China to sink into a semicolonial, semifeudal society. Thus, the national minorities within China were prevented from emerging as modern nations despite their economic and linguistic unity, their shared customs and culture, and their common habitats. There is nothing remarkable about this particular historical phenomenon. Today, when each of China's nationalities has already attained liberation, the question is not for them to form together a capitalist nation but rather, in general, of having them evolve themselves one by one as socialist nations.

The distinctive attributes of a nation, as represented by modern scientific research, are commonality of language, culture, customs, and historical tradition; a certain stage of socioeconomic development; and a certain pattern of territorial distribution. But for many comparatively small nationalities, it is extremely difficult to ascertain whether they actually constitute a nation or whether they simply have distinct names of their own. This is due to the fact that these peoples, defeated in their wars of resistance against the Han, Mongols, Manchus, or other comparatively large nations which governed China at various historical times, were persecuted and scattered, and for too long a time such isolated groups had no contact with one another. Without any economic development, moreover, a national consciousness could not be awakened among them; and when long retarded in a clan or tribal milieu, they habitually used their own name for their particular subgroup. Thus, the Lolo (Yi) are variously called La-hu, La-hsi, Li-su, Ha-ni, etc. Then again, Chuang or T'ai people who fled to Yunnan and Kweichow after their defeat were called Nung, Sha, Pu-yi, etc., according to their different locations. Sometimes they were arbitrarily given different names by the Han: for instance, the Lolos were called "barbarians" and the Ching-p'o "mountaintop people." Furthermore, there were other names for the Han people, such as

"Chinese";[5] for the Mongols, "Tartars"; and for the Manchus, "Nuchen." Any reunification of single nations with different names must be decided on the basis of the wishes of the peoples themselves, but this question cannot be resolved at once. Once the alienation of the nationalities is overcome, however, I believe that the various groups of an originally single nationality will come to "recognize their kinship" and "join clans" on the basis of their basically similar languages, cultures, and customs, and then select a name for the whole people. But if for whatever reason they wish to retain their individual names, their desire will be respected. If nationalities with different names have been closely connected in the past, or have related languages, or have been economically interdependent due to adjoining habitats, a basis would thereby exist for their free selection of a common name. Similarly, if there is a unified national name but not, in practice, a similarity of language and the other factors, the people in question must be permitted to decide their name freely, either retaining or changing the old one.

The expression we used in the past, "the Chinese people,"[6] meant all of China's nationalities. Thus, there is nothing wrong with using this name, but the expression, "the peoples of China,"[7] is even more appropriate. This is because the term, "the Chinese people," may be misunderstood as meaning that the Chinese People's Republic consists of a single nationality.

5 The character used here is *hua* ("flowery").

6 "Chung-hua min-tsu."

7 "Chung-kuo ko min-tsu."

Apart from the Hui and the Manchus, who employ Han writing and speech, the Mongols, Tibetans, Miao, Yi, Uighur, Koreans, Kazakhs, Sibo, T'ai, Ching-p'o, Li-su, and others among the national minorities of our country have their own languages and literatures, though in some cases the written languages are still incomplete.[8] There are also some national minorities which lack a system of writing, although they have their own spoken languages.

*The national minorities of our country have been strongly influenced by religious beliefs; the religions with the most numerous adherents are Islam and Buddhism.* Among the masses in national minority areas which border on neighboring countries [to the south], moreover, there are a great many Catholics and Protestants. Counted as Moslems are the Hui, Uighur, Kazakh, Uzbek, Kirghiz, Tung-hsiang, Tajik, Tatar, Salar, and Pao-an: these ten peoples account for more than eight million people in a total national minority population of over thirty-five million. The five peoples considered Buddhists are the Tibetan, Mongol, T'u, Yü-ku, and T'ai,[9] with a total population of more than 4,600,000. The two groups together represent over one-third of our country's national minority population. There are nu-

[8] Only the Mongols, Tibetans, Uighurs, and Koreans can seriously be said to possess literatures, though other nationalities possess more or less crude means of writing their languages, often in connection with religious practices: some of these employ Chinese characters, while systems based on the Latin or Arabic alphabets are used by others; the T'ai employ a script derived from India. Cf. Chapter 3, note 7.

[9] The T'ai follow Hinayana Buddhism, which has little in common with the Lamaism of the Tibetans, Mongols, etc.

merous temples and mosques in these national minority areas, and the number of persons for whom the teaching of religion is a vocation is correspondingly large. In the national minority areas that are predominantly Buddhist, there are, according to incomplete statistics, more than 5,000 temples, 3,000 living Buddhas, and 320,000 lamas, while among the Moslems there are some 40,000 mosques and more than 100,000 imams and mullahs. In addition, there are groups of Catholics and Protestants among the Miao, Yi, Ching-p'o, Nu, Ch'iu,[10] K'awa, and other nationalities. Although the other national minorities do not have systematized religions, for the most part they retain their comparatively primitive polytheism; religious superstition is also widespread.

All the religions of the national minorities, except Catholicism and Protestantism which entered China comparatively late, have long histories.[11] They have strongly influenced the political, economic, and cultural development of these peoples, and developed deep roots among the masses. The socioeconomic backwardness of some of the national minority areas as compared with the Han areas, coupled with the system of nationalities oppression which lasted for a long time, created advantageous circumstances for the propagation and development of religion in  the national minority areas; and

10 "Ch'iu" is equivalent to "Nung."

11 On account of its connections with imperialism, Christianity in China is accorded less tolerance than are Buddhism and Islam. The position of the latter is further strengthened because most of the countries of Asia which China seeks to influence are either Buddhist or Islamic. See Francis P. Jones, "The Christian Church in Communist China," *Far Eastern Survey* (December 1955), pp. 184–188.

this penetration of religious influences greatly hindered the political, economic, and cultural development of the national minority areas. The reactionary ruling groups either attacked or made use of the religions of the national minorities, but whichever it was, religious influence became progressively more widespread and penetrating. The religions which the reactionary rulers sought to use naturally flourished, while the religions being attacked, far from being weakened, were actually strengthened as a result of their resistance. Many national minorities, in their struggles against nationalities oppression, often raised the banner of "protect religion," and made the bond of religion an important unifying factor for their own nationality.

Buddhism and Islam, which have great numbers of adherents among the national minorities of our country, are both universal religions that have strongly influenced many countries of Asia and Africa, where they have sometimes become "state religions."

In view of these circumstances, the religious question in national minority areas is closely related to the national question as a whole.

*In the course of historical developments over a long period of time, the various nationalities of our country together brought into being our great motherland; through a long period of contact there occurred economic cooperation and cultural exchange among the nationalities. Moreover, on a great many occasions they united in combating foreign invaders and in resisting reactionary rulers. During the past hundred years the forcible encroachments on China by the imperialists brought about*

*an intimate and indestructible identification of the des-*
*tinies of each of the nationalities. For these reasons,*
*they all joined together in forming the great, united*
*family of China's nationalities — the indivisible Peo-*
*ple's Republic of China. It must be admitted, however,*
*that for a very long time there was no unity among the*
*nationalities.* Prior to the moment that the rule of the
Kuomintang reactionary clique over the whole country
was smashed by the Chinese people, the situation of the
various nationalities in our country remained unequal.
The evils of the system of nationalities oppression continued, with successive generations occupying positions
of authority within the reactionary ruling cliques of a
number of nationalities. Most important of these was the
reactionary ruling clique of the Han people, which also
dominated the reactionary ruling class of the time. With
this centralized feudal system, they not only cruelly oppressed the people of the nationalities in question, pro-
voking discord among the nationalities and causing
mutual distrust and animosity, but they even more
cruelly oppressed other peoples, thus robbing the national minorities of their political, economic, and educational rights and long delaying the development that
was their due. There was thus established discord and
alienation among the nationalities. Moreover, the phenomenon of the splitting up of nationalities appeared.
In face of the oppression of the imperialists who came
from outside, however, China's nationalities strove to
continue to develop the interrelationship formed by their
long historical contact and opposition to common
enemies; and while the system of nationalities oppres-

sion inherited from China's history remained, they clearly recognized that "nationalities unity" was in the interests of all the peoples of China, whereas "nationalities division" only served the greedy schemes of the world imperialists and meant for all the peoples of China a continuation in the sad old way as slaves of world colonialism.[12] In this the nationalities of China were obliged to take the path of establishing a powerful, united, national state, thereby eliminating alienation, strengthening trust, uniting the strength of all the nationalities to achieve victory against imperialism, feudalism, and bureaucrat capitalism, and together attain liberation; rather than choose the path of the division of nationalities, each going its own way, which would result in perpetual slavery. The fates of all of China's nationalities are interconnected in this way. Therefore, they have experienced every national revolutionary struggle from the time of the Opium War, until finally, under the leadership of the Chinese Communist Party, there appeared the united front of all of China's nationalities, with the Han at the center: "the peoples of China have united."[13] In the course of China's revolutionary struggle, relations of mutual help among the nationalities definitely continued to expand, but the enmity and alienation inherited from the past sometimes still showed

[12] This is the focus of the Chinese Communist rewriting of Chinese history in relation to the national question. In fact, the national minorities did not unite with the Han Chinese in resisting the imperialists: they were, on the contrary, only too ready to take advantage of the imperialist "encroachments" to try to shake off Han Chinese domination.

[13] A phrase used by Mao Tse-tung at the time of Liberation.

itself and had the effect of destroying nationalities unity.

This, then, is the question which exists of the relationship among China's nationalities, and also the national question that the Chinese revolution has to solve. As Comrade Liu Shao-ch'i said in his political report at the Eighth National Congress of the Chinese Communist Party [in 1956]: "To dispose correctly of the national minority question is a very important task in our national work." And this task is connected with the question of whether or not socialist society can be smoothly established in our country.

# CHAPTER TWO

# The Correct Way of Resolving
# the National Question

There are two contrasting ways of resolving the question of nationalities:[1] one is the way of national oppression which, regardless of whether it takes the form of "kindness" or repression, amounts to a policy of assimilation and extermination of the national minorities. This is the way of the reactionary regimes of the past, among which the most extreme was the Kuomintang clique of Chiang Kai-shek. It does not admit the existence of national minorities within the frontiers of China, but, on the contrary, looks upon the nationalities as merely branches — or clans — of the Han people.[2] This is the

[1] As the author's discussion turns from theory to practice, I have tended to translate "min-tsu wen-t'i" as "nationalities question" rather than as "national question," for it is only in theory that the minorities have real status as nations.

[2] This is the conventional Chinese notion, namely, to think of all the inhabitants of China as comprising a single nation. Thus, the standard *Tz'u-hai* dictionary (1925 edition) gives the Chinese people *(Chung-hua min-tsu)* as an example of "nation" *(min-tsu)*, which it says is "A group of people united by similarities of blood, way of life, language, religion, customs, and so forth." The Anglo-Saxons are offered as another example. No doubt one of the great obstacles to a broad acceptance among Han Chinese of CCP nationalities policy is this

way of splitting up the nationalities; this is the discredited way followed by generation after generation of feudal rulers (including the Chiang Kai-shek clique, which represents the feudal landowning and bureaucrat-capitalist class); this is a blind alley which we absolutely can never follow again. The other way is that of the equality of nationalities: this is the way of the Communist Party. It recognizes the complete equality of the nationalities of China regardless of whether they are advanced or backward, large or small. And regional autonomy is put into effect in areas where the minorities live together, granting them the right to manage their own local affairs. This is the way of nationalities unity; this is the bright way indicated by Marxism-Leninism.

In order to elucidate the importance of the national question in the Chinese revolution and the correctness of the nationalities policy of the Chinese Communist Party,

---

contrary cast of mind, which, though totally lacking scientific foundation, has deep psychological and historical roots.

Writing in 1942–1943, Chiang Kai-shek said that China's development had been retarded because the Ch'ing dynasty (1644–1911) had not treated "the five clans" (Han, Manchu, Mongol, Tibetan, Hui) equally. In fact, Ch'ing policy discriminated in favor of China's non-Han peoples, limiting Han Chinese colonization and commercial activity in the frontier regions: it is this brake on the assimilation of China's non-Han peoples to which Chiang must have been objecting. See Chiang Kai-shek, *China's Destiny* (New York, 1947), p. 47. In Kuomintang literature generally, the minorities are referred to as *pien-chiang min-tsu* or "frontier peoples." Both the Nationalists and the Communists claim faithfulness to the ideas of Sun Yat-sen with regard to the question of China's nationalities, and justifiably so, for Sun's ideas on this subject changed from an earlier assimilationist attitude (as expressed in *The Three Principles of the People*) to a Leninist approach after he had become committed to a united front with the Communists (as shown in the Manifesto [endorsed by Sun] of the First National Congress of the Kuomintang [1924]),

we must go back a little to the historical development
of the Chinese Communist Party's work with the nationalities, including the great contribution made by the
national minority peoples themselves to the Chinese
revolution.

*The Chinese Communist Party has consistently recog-
nized the nationalities question as being one of the major
questions of the Chinese revolution and the liberation of
the national minorities as being a part of the liberation
of the Chinese people.*   Thus, it sought, externally, the
throwing back of the imperialists who had encroached
upon us, and, internally, the liberation and equality of
all nationalities. This was always an important policy
of the Chinese Communist Party in leading the Chinese
people's democratic revolution. The Manifesto of the
Second Congress of the Chinese Communist Party contained proposals concerning the principle of nationalism.
It proposed that: China proper (including Manchuria)
be a true democratic republic and that the three regions
of Mongolia, Tibet, and Turkestan be autonomous,
forming democratic self-governing regions; China,
Mongolia, Tibet, and Turkestan would then unite on the
basis of their own free will, thereby establishing a Chinese federal republic.[3] At the time of the first domestic
revolutionary war in 1927, several Party representatives,
including Hsieh Ch'u-nu, Ch'ü Ch'iu-pai, and other

[3] Cf. *A Documentary History of Chinese Communism* by Conrad
Brandt, Benjamin Schwartz, and John K. Fairbank (Cambridge,
Massachusetts, 1952), p. 64. This general line was repeated at the
Sixth Congress in 1928, as well as on other occasions, as noted in
the bibliography.

comrades, expounded the Party's nationalities policy in public writings.[4] Moreover, the "Draft Constitution" promulgated by the First Soviet Congress in November 1931 contained resolutions concerning nationalities policy, including the fundamental rules for national self-determination.[5] In the August 1935 "Decisions of the Central Committee on the political situation and our tasks following the linking-up of the First and Fourth Front Armies," it was pointed out that bringing the national minorities under the leadership of the Chinese Communist Party and the actual Chinese people's revolutionary government "will be of decisive significance on the road ahead to the victory of the Chinese people's revolution."[6] Even during the most difficult time of the Chinese people's democratic revolution — during the twenty-five thousand *li* Long March — this great banner was not lowered. While the Chinese people's fraternal forces were traversing the territory of the national minorities, the Chinese Communist Party consistently manifested an attitude of equality and friendship toward

[4] I am not familiar with these writings. In January 1926, Ch'ü Ch'iu-pai (a senior member of the CCP from the time of its founding) gave a series of four lectures at Shanghai University on "The National Question Today" (Ting Ching-t'ang and Wen Ts'ao, *Chronological Bibliography of the Works of Chü Ch'iu-pai* [Shanghai: People's Publishing House, 1959], p. 34), but I have not been able to consult them.

[5] See Appendix B.

[6] An earlier Central Committee meeting, held in January 1935, had established Mao Tse-tung as the leader of the CCP. At the August meeting, Mao's position was unsuccessfully challenged by Chang Kuo-t'ao, leader of the Fourth Front Army. Both meetings were held during the Long March, the first in Kweichow and the second on the Tibetan marches of Szechwan. So far as is known, there has been no serious schism within the CCP since the August meeting.

the national minorities. Moreover, they helped them establish popular governments of their own. As a result, a profound impression was left with the national minority regions in the southwest. After the Chinese Communist Party had led the Chinese people's fraternal forces northward to the north Shensi revolutionary base area, it issued a statement to the people of Inner Mongolia. Issued in the name of the actual people's revolutionary government on 20 December 1935, it clearly said: the task of the Chinese people's revolution is not only to achieve the liberation of the entire Chinese people from imperialist and warlord oppression, but even more to struggle for the liberation of the "small and weak peoples" within the country. It was noted in the statement that only if we and the people of Inner Mongolia struggle together could our common enemies, the Japanese imperialists and Chiang Kai-shek, be quickly defeated; similarly, it was only in common struggle with us that the Inner Mongolian people could avoid national destruction and take the road of national rejuvenation. At the same time, several practical suggestions were made to them:

(1) Recognizing that the original boundaries of Inner Mongolia's six leagues, twenty-four divisions, forty-nine banners, the two divisions of Chahar and Tumet, and three special districts of Ninghsia have all been extensively altered, whether in terms of *hsien* jurisdiction or of pasturelands, all must be restored to the people of Inner Mongolia and this must be done in accord with the leadership of Inner Mongolia. The names and administrations of the three provinces of Jehol, Chahar, and Suiyuan must be abolished:[7] other people cannot

---

[7] Established by the Nationalist government in 1929 as part — or so

seize and lyingly divest the Inner Mongolian people of their lands. (2) We recognize the right of the people of Inner Mongolia to decide all questions pertaining to themselves, for no one has the right to forcefully interfere with the way of life, religious observances, etc., of the Inner Mongolian people. At the same time, the people of Inner Mongolia are free to build a system of their own choosing; they are at liberty to develop their own livelihood, establish their own government, unite in a federation with other peoples, or to make themselves entirely separate. In a word, the people are sovereign, and all nationalities are equal. (3) As for the Han, Hui, Tibetan, Manchu, and other peoples found in Inner Mongolia, democracy must be fostered among them in accordance with the principal of national equality and they must be treated as the equals of the Mongols; moreover, they must have freedom to use their own spoken and written languages as well as freedom of religion and residence. (4) The Pa-tu-wan area occupied by Tsing Yo-hsin and the area, including two salt mines, seized by Kao Shih-hsin, must be returned immediately to the people of Inner Mongolia.[8] Furthermore, places close to the Great Wall such as Ning-t'iao-liang, An-pien, Ting-pien,[9] and others must be made into commercial centers and trade developed between the two sides. (5) Neither our Workers' and Peasants' Red Army partisans nor their armed units have any plan for advancing into the pastures, but you likewise must not allow troops of the Chinese warlords or the Japanese imperialists to cross your grasslands and attack us, thereby hastening your own destruction. We are willing to conclude with you a defensive and offensive alliance and struggle for the overthrow of our common enemies.

---

it has been generally interpreted — of an assimilationist drive. At the same time, eastern Tibet was put under Chinese administration as the provinces of Tsinghai and Sikang.

[8] I have not succeeded in identifying these incidents. Salt was of great importance to the Mongols, and the Chinese Communists hoped to reap political rewards by making it easier for them to attain the salt they needed.

[9] These three towns, all in Shensi Province, are shown on Map 2.

The statement also said:

To sum up, if, not wishing to become stateless, you will really recognize the need for Mongol independence and decide to oppose Japanese imperialism as well as Chiang Kai-shek and other Chinese warlords, then we, with good intentions, can extend real aid to you, regardless of whether your leaders are of the nobility or the common people.[10]

A statement with a similar theme was addressed to the Hui people on 25 May 1936. It said:

. . . (1) Our fundamental policy of national self-determination extends to the local affairs of the Hui people. In all Hui areas, free and independent political authority established by the Hui people themselves will decide all matters relating to politics, economics, religion, customs and habits, morals, education, and so forth. Wherever Hui people are in a minority, whether in large regions, in districts, or in villages, they shall, on the basis of the principle of the equality of nationalities, establish Hui people's autonomous governments and manage their own affairs. (2) In accordance with the principle of religious freedom, we protect the position of mosques and imams and absolutely guarantee religious freedom for the Hui people. (3) Possessing arms is a necessary condition for being a free and independent nation. Joining with the total armed strength of the Hui people themselves, we can, through mutual help, establish an independent "Hui people's anti-Japanese army." We want to see the forces of the Hui people become an important part of the joint anti-Japanese army. (4) By abolishing the oppressive taxes and miscellaneous levies of the militarists, official cliques, and militia, the living standard of the Hui people will be improved. (5) . . . Develop the Hui people's education, establish Hui language newspapers, and raise the

[10] The Japanese were already actively penetrating Inner Mongolia by the time this statement was made, and there was evidence that some Mongols were sympathetic to Japanese-sponsored "autonomy."

political and cultural level of the Hui people. (6) Let a close relationship develop between the two great nations of the Hui and the Han, and overthrow Japanese imperialism and the nation-selling Han traitors. (7) Uniting with Turkey, Outer Mongolia, the Soviet Union, and other peoples and states sympathetic with the complete liberation of all the peoples of China, together oppose Japan.[11]

During 1940, in April and July, respectively, summaries of the Hui and Mongol questions were made by the office of the Secretary of the Central Committee. Both sought to strengthen, in opposition to Japan, the unity of the nationalities which, historically, had been alienated and oppressed and brought into opposition with the Han people by the reactionary ruling class (especially the Kuomintang administration). On the basis of these summaries, the Northwest Work Committee decided to make known the seriousness of the nationalities question at that time and to expose the plot of the imperialists to use contradictions between China's nationalities in order to stir up dissension among them. It was then recognized that the key to the uniting of the national minorities against Japan was to have a correct policy — that, namely, of simultaneously transforming the Kuomintang government's position of great Hanism and overcoming the tendency toward narrow nationalism on the part of the national minorities, who would then put faith in our policy, reducing and gradually eliminating their prejudice toward us. We must rely on the principle of nationalities equality in order to eliminate contradictions

[11] At the time, there was strong pan-Islamic (and thus pro-Turkey) feeling among the estimated ten million Moslems in China's northwest. See Edgar Snow, *Red Star Over China* (London, 1937), pp. 321 ff.

among the nationalities; to give the national minorities democratic rights; to let them manage their own internal affairs; to respect their religious beliefs, spoken and written languages, and customs and habits; to assist them in improving their economic conditions of life; to help them train cadres and establish armed forces; etc. Moreover, many practical consequences flowed from these principles. During the Anti-Japanese War, the Chinese Communist Party frequently called for, and in liberated areas actually carried out, the policy of national regional autonomy. In the section on "The National Minority Question" of his 1945 work, *On Coalition Government*, Comrade Mao Tse-tung made the matter still more clear and definite by declaring:

The broad masses, including the leading personalities who are connected with the masses, of all national minorities must be assisted in the liberation and development of their governments, economies, and cultures and in the establishment of their own military units to protect the rights of the masses. Their spoken and written languages, customs and habits, and religious beliefs must be respected.

All of the foregoing makes it clear that throughout its history the Chinese Communist Party has always concerned itself with the national question.

Why do some people take the view that the national question in China, during the revolutionary period of New Democracy, was of a different character than in the Soviet Union?[12] There are several reasons for this misunderstanding. While China is a multinational state, the chief nationality is the Han, who represent more than

[12] For an explanation of "New Democracy," see Chapter Four, note 5.

90 per cent of the total population and who, on the whole, are politically, economically, culturally, and in other respects more advanced than the minority nationalities. There is a big difference between this situation and the situation of the nationalities in Russia before the October revolution. In the Russia of that time, the number of Russians did not even represent half the total population, whereas the population of the other nationalities together made up more than half the total. Furthermore, some of these other nationalities were superior to the Russians in their economic and cultural development. Again, the high tide of the national movement rose at an early date on account of the cruel oppression of the Czar. In the early makeup of the Chinese revolution, on the other hand, aside from the Outer Mongolian independence movement that was launched at the end of the Ch'ing dynasty, there were very few large-scale national movements of liberation, although the ceaseless uprisings of the other national minorities against the reactionary ruling class continued as before. Under these dissimilar circumstances, the national problem within China, as it developed in the course of the Chinese revolution (especially at the beginning), was not, naturally, characterized by mutual trust to the extent that it was in the Russian revolution. Furthermore, China's national democratic revolution emerged first in Han areas and especially in the south and along the coast. These regions are comparatively distant from the important national minority areas, and the ties with the national minority peoples were consequently few. Another, still weightier consideration derived from the

leading revolutionary task of the time, which was to carry forward the anti-imperialist, antifeudal struggle: thus, from the beginning, the problem was to liberate all the nationalities and the country from the oppression of foreign imperialism, and the chief contradiction for the Chinese revolution to resolve at that time was the contradiction between imperialism and the great mass of the Chinese people. These circumstances have caused some people to assume falsely that an internal national question was not present. The actual circumstances of the historical development of the revolution tell us that the Chinese Communist Party seriously viewed the internal nationalities question in the past and that it has consistently recognized that the national question within the frontiers of China is a very serious one.

*As the Chinese revolution has evolved, so has the national question; the tasks imposed by the national question vary according to the way the revolution develops.* During the New Democracy phase of the revolution, the Chinese Communist Party called for an equal alliance of the Han people with the people of all nationalities within the frontiers of China so that together they could oppose imperialist encroachment and the feudalism and bureaucrat-capitalism represented by the Kuomintang and overthrow the regime of the feudal landlords and bureaucrat-capitalist class. These tasks were basically achieved with the establishment of the Chinese People's Republic on 1 October 1949. Accordingly, within the sphere of the whole state, the relations among our nationalities have already been fundamentally altered.

With each nationality in the country having achieved liberation, with the system of nationalities oppression basically abolished, and with the nationalities of our country having already entered the era of nationalities equality, can "national liberation" still be regarded as the task of each national minority? Of course, it cannot. Since the system of nationalities oppression no longer exists, the aim of national liberation has already been achieved. If it is said that people of certain nationalities still suffer from oppression and slavery and still have the task of "liberation," that does not imply the oppression of small and weak nationalities by a large one; rather, it has to do with the continuing existence of the system of oppression — of the slave system and the feudal system — within certain nationalities. If the people of each national minority seek complete liberation, they do so in order to eliminate their internal systems of oppression and to develop their government, economy, and culture; there is no other question involved. This concept must be made absolutely clear, for otherwise individual reactionary elements within certain nationalities might take advantage of it. Such is the real situation, but we must still give heed to the vestiges of alienation and discrimination among the nationalities caused by the reactionary ruling classes of the past, and especially to the alienation between each of the nationalities and the Han, and to the discriminatory treatment of the national minorities during the era of government by the reactionary Han ruling class, both of which have become deeply imbedded in society. Therefore, we must, throughout the whole country in the first period of being liberated, universally employ methods that strengthen nationalities unity and dissipate nationalities alienation; we must also promote mutual respect and oppose discrimination. Since the continuation of this alienation and discrimination is of no value to the people of any of the nationalities, it can only serve our common enemies — the imperialists and the reactionary Kuomintang clique. To facilitate the thoroughgoing resolution of this problem that has had such a long history, the Chinese Communist Party, basing itself on Marxist-Leninist theory concerning the national question, advocates collective responsibility on the part of both the whole country and the people of each nationality concerning the domestic nationalities question in today's transition stage.[13] This obligation is to strengthen the unity of the motherland and the solidarity of all the nationalities, secure the defense of the state, and together establish a great socialist family of the motherland; within the great united family of the motherland, to protect all the equal rights of each nationality and carry out national regional autonomy; in the development of national affairs and in the creation of an intimate national harmony, to develop steadily the political, economic, and cultural affairs of each nationality (including firm progress in the necessary socialist reform); to eliminate the real inequalities among the nationalities; and to make the backward nationalities attain the level of the advanced nationalities, finally making the transition to socialist society. This responsibility of the Chinese Communist Party with respect to the nationalities question was reflected in the 1949 Common

[13] For an explanation of "transition stage," see Chapter Four, note 5.

Program of the Chinese People's Political Consultative Conference. In Chapter Six of the Common Program it is said: "All nationalities within the frontiers of China are equal. They are to practice unity and mutual help. . . . Acts of discrimination, oppression, and division contrary to the unity of nationalities are forbidden." "Regional autonomy must be put into practice in areas where national minorities live together, with various organs of self-government being established according to the size of the population and the area inhabited by the nationality. Nationalities which live in scattered places or within other autonomous regions must all have the requisite number of representatives in the organs of political power where they reside." It is also stated in the Common Program: ". . . the People's Government must help the broad mass of the people of each nationality to develop their political, economic, cultural, and educational facilities." Chapter Five, as well as the Preamble, of the Constitution passed by the first session of the First National People's Congress in 1954, aside from continuing to speak in this genuine spirit, also contained a number of practical regulations concerning nationalities equality, the self-governing rights of national regional autonomy, and other matters that marked an advance over the Common Program.[14]

*Therefore, the principle of nationalities equality is not merely fully reflected in the Constitution of our country; it is also a special characteristic of the Constitution.* To safeguard the equal rights of the national minorities, the

[14] Relevant passages from the Common Program and the Constitution are given in Appendix C.

government of our country has, during the past several years, promulgated "General Regulations for National Regional Autonomy in the Chinese People's Republic," "Resolution Concerning the Protection of Equal Rights Enjoyed by All Groups of National Minorities Living in Dispersed Places," "Instructions Concerning the Disposition of Designations, Place Names, Stone Inscriptions, and Votive Tablets which Manifest a Discriminatory or Insulting Attitude Toward the National Minorities," and others in a series of decisions, and also furthered nationalities equality through mass education and protected the equal rights of the national minorities.[15]

*Why have we consistently advocated "the safeguarding of the territory and the equality of all rights for each nationality within the country"?*   It is because:

1.   *The equality of nationalities is a fundamental internationalist tenet of Communist Party members.* Unless equality is first achieved with respect to all rights, then the alienation, suspicion, and discrimination among nationalities which have been inherited from the past cannot be eliminated. Inasmuch as nationalities alienation has developed over a long historical period, this aliena-

[15] The first two items, translated, respectively, as the "General Program of the People's Republic of China for the Implementation of Regional Autonomy for Nationalities" and "Decisions on the Protection of the Right of All Scattered National Minority People to National Equality," both of which were adopted by the Central People's Government in 1952, may be found in *Policy Toward Nationalities of the Chinese People's Republic* (Peking: Foreign Languages Press, 1953). The third item, concerning place names, etc., is among the *Collected Documents on Nationalities Policy* (Min-tsu cheng-ts'e wen-hsien wei-pien) published by the People's Publishing House, Peking, 1953.

tion psychology is still very profound: it cannot be thoroughly rooted out in a short time or by carrying out a few measures; rather, a long and difficult period of work is required for success. This is certainly not a light or easily managed problem. But if things do not go well in areas where it is very manifest, force will be used; in areas where it is not so evident or where it is buried, today's exhortations will not suffice to make it completely disappear.

2.    *The historical call of the working class is for the liberation of all mankind, and Marx recognized that a people which oppresses another people is not really free.*[16] The working people of the Han nationality help the people of the national minorities; at the same time, the minority peoples help the Han people. It must be recognized that this "help" is mutual. By contributing to the strength of national unity and the security of the national defense, each of China's national minorities has thereby supported the progress of the motherland in the building of socialism, and the contribution of each nationality is magnified by the efforts of the Han people. This kind of mutual help reconciles the interests of each nationality with the interests of all of China's nationalities taken together.

3.    *The national question is a part of the more general problem of the proletarian revolution, and Marxism-*

16 Marx wrote in 1869, with reference to the persecution of the Irish by the English, that "A people which enslaves another people forges its own chains." See Ralph Fox, *Marx, Engels and Lenin on the Irish Revolution* (London, 1932), p. 31.

*Leninism recognizes that the national question should be served by the class struggle.* The class reality of the national question, taking the peasant question as its main feature, has to do with the question of the relationship between the working class and the peasantry of each nationality, and the question of the alliance of the working class with the peasantry. This is because "the peasant question is the foundation and the central focus of the national question." It is also said: "The national question is actually the peasant question" (Stalin). This stems from the following:

*i.* After the October revolution the national question merged with the national colonial question — the question of the peoples of colonial and dependent countries attaining liberation from imperialist oppression. On the basis of the dominant position which monopoly capital assumed with the development of capitalism to the stage of imperialism, the capitalist class in imperialist countries absolutely never took the part of national liberators: on the contrary, they turned into the greatest national oppressors. Especially after the First World War, the capitalist class in these countries deepened and expanded their oppression and plundering of the countries of small and weak peoples. For this reason, the national question was joined with the general question of the quest for liberation on the part of each nationality in the colonial and semicolonial countries. The interests of the national liberation movement and the proletarian revolution became united in their opposition to the colonial system, and the struggles of both became parts of the socialist revolution, *ii.* All of the oppressed nations were economically backward, and the largest part of their populations was the peasantry. The peasants make up the basic forces in the national movement: without these supporting ranks of the peasants, there could not be a strong national movement.

With a few exceptions, China's national minorities lagged behind the Han people in their level of social and economic development. Some of them still had the slave system; the mode of production characteristic of primitive society remained among some others. But as for the bulk of the population, the most important producing element among the national minorities is the peasantry. Therefore, any failure on our part to manage the national question properly will have repercussions for the worker-peasant alliance. But the national question is not the same thing as the peasant question, and the two cannot be simply lumped together, the disposition of the peasant question being regarded as sufficient; while contradictions among nationalities are really class contradictions, nationality contradictions and class contradictions should not be confusedly talked about as the same thing.[17] In our past nationalities work, some people have paid exclusive attention to certain areas of class conflict while ignoring the contradiction among nationalities. This makes it possible for incorrect policies to be developed. According to our analysis, most of the national minorities are differentiated along class lines. In gen-

[17] By means of this flight into Marxist-Leninist theory, the author seeks to demonstrate the compatibility of Chinese Communist policy with Stalinism, rather than to illuminate a specifically Chinese situation.

eral, moreover, these class differentiations are quite obvious; only in a few instances is class differentiation still not fully apparent. Thus, among those nationalities whose class differentiation is comparatively pronounced, nationalities that had experienced alienation from and even conflict with other nationalities brought on by the reactionary rulers of the past, the upper-strata reactionary elements even today are capable of exploiting this "national alienation" and "national struggle," which are in fact only disguises for the class struggle carried on by the reactionaries. This kind of dissension-sowing even influences the outlook of the laboring people, whose political consciousness has not yet attained the requisite level. For example, when land reform was carried out in areas where national minorities and Han people live mixed together, the national minorities were frequently violent during the land-reform struggle: however, if Han masses in struggling against a national minority landlord became violent, the national minority masses would not be satisfied: they would demand that a Han landlord be dragged before the distribution struggle. This inclination on the part of the national minority masses is not explicable in terms of the antilandlord struggle alone, for to some extent it also reveals the feelings of certain nationalities. These feelings are understandable. For there were also areas in which the influence of great Hanist remnants was felt during the distribution of the fruits of the land-reform struggle, and so it happened that the national minorities did not receive fair treatment in the distribution. If conditions in areas where national minorities are scattered are like this, the situation in places where they are concentrated can be yet more easily visualized. In view of these conditions, it is evident that, when working in national minority areas, we must always maintain a sober attitude. For if only the high level of mass emotion is taken into account, and attention paid to nationalities alienation alone, then some positive elements will be misguided into expanding the appetite of the masses. This could lead our work into oversimplification and inflexibility, produce dissatisfaction on the part of the masses, and imperil the revolutionary cause.

*Why does the Chinese Communist Party especially want to strengthen nationalities solidarity and at the same time secure the unity of the motherland?* There are several reasons for this.

Nationalities solidarity is a necessary condition for the creation of the motherland just as it is for the collective development of all the nationalities. We cannot conceive of an internally disunited country successfully becoming established. Due to the ill will among the nationalities caused by the reactionary rulers' oppression, the history of China has been marked by the frequent occurrence of wars among the nationalities as well as by continuous peasant wars. The war and disorder among the nationalities which, with fluctuating intensity, had lasted for such a long historical period, was resolved in a fundamental way only following the establishment of the new China, when the nationalities of our country were introduced to the idea of political unity and to the benefits of increasing their mutual solidarity. In this manner, a united motherland was properly secured.

While talking about this spirit of unity and solidarity among the nationalities, however, we must not disregard those divisions that continue to exist today among the nationalities — such as different characteristics, different historical situations, different stages of social development, different class relationships, different economic and cultural levels, different levels of awareness and sincerity, different degrees of historically inherited alienation, and so on. If these differences are disregarded, it will not be possible to discern the myriad schemes of the imperialists and their running dogs to spread discord and contention among the national minorities: those inhabiting the frontier regions have been particularly exposed, and have even been subject to constant intimidation of this sort. Such a lack of perception on our part would lead to political mistakes that, in turn, would make it impossible to satisfactorily resolve the question of nationalities unity. It would then be difficult to secure internal peace and safeguard the national defense.

In the present-day world, the American imperialists continue at the head of the colonialist camp. They stubbornly oppose lasting peace and people's democracy and cling to their policies of encroachment and colonialism. If we cannot satisfactorily unite the national minorities within our borders, this might have the effect of pushing them out of the great family of the Chinese People's Republic, handing them over to imperialism, and causing slavery to be imposed upon them. This is not the way for Communists. Besides, severing the bonds among the nationalities would not, as we have already pointed out, be in the interests either of the Han people or of the national minority people. It follows that to continue being cautious and suspicious is not in the interests of the people of any nationality. This would provide an opportunity for the dissension-sowing schemes of the imperialists and their Kuomintang running dogs. We must bear this warning constantly in mind and not allow the enemy any advantage.

It is only by fundamentally implementing the principle of national equality that the objectives of unity, mutual help, and trust among the nationalities can be reached.

The experience of the Soviet Union provides us with an example: after revolutionary successes spanning forty years, they still emphasize the need to strengthen the unity of the Soviet nationalities. Yet there are those who take the view that the nationalities question no longer exists in post-Liberation China, or at least that it has basically been overcome. The two positions are objectively irreconcilable.

*Why does the Chinese Communist Party, with respect to the tasks concerning the national question in the transition period, give prominence to safeguarding the unity of the motherland and nationalities solidarity rather than the principle constantly emphasized by Lenin — that of "national self-determination"?* In the first place, as we know, the Chinese Communist Party, on the basis of the Marxist-Leninist formulation of the national question, consistently advocated self-determination and federalism from the day the Party was founded until the period of the Anti-Japanese War. It was only with the period of China's third revolutionary war that these slogans ceased to be emphasized. This was because, as already related, during the hundred years and more since the Opium War, and especially during the past thirty-odd years, the bonds of mutual help among the nationalities of our country were further strengthened, rather than weakened, in the revolutionary struggle of their respective peoples, together, against foreign oppression. Led and instructed by the Chinese Communist Party, the people of each nationality had already greatly heightened their internationalist and patriotic consciousness, greatly changed and transcended their original situation of mutual antagonism, and gradually formed bonds of equality, unity, mutual help, and cooperation as a basis for realizing common political aims and interests. Therefore, the establishment of a united, multinational state was the desire of the great bulk of the people of all nationalities in our country. It was in accord with this noble wish of the people of all nationalities that the Chinese Communist Party advocated the carrying out of the principle of nationalities equality and national regional autonomy within the unity of the great family of the motherland and discontinued emphasizing the slogan of national self-determination and federalism.[18] Consequently, the question of national division or national separation does not even arise in present-day circumstances: such schemes would inevitably meet with the violent opposition of the broad masses of all nationalities. Particularly, in their common experience of long, bitter struggle in which much blood was spilt and by means of which

[18] The real reason for this change is that Mao Tse-tung did not favor federalism for China, as his predecessors in the CCP leadership had.

was established their own united, great family of the
motherland — the Chinese People's Republic — the people of all nationalities had tasted the benefits of the
policy of nationalities equality and national regional autonomy. After all this, the suggestions of "national division" and "national separation" would clearly be
unacceptable to the great bulk of the people of all nationalities in our country. Anyone still wishing to advance
this slogan could only expect to find himself completely
isolated. Furthermore, "national self-determination" is
not to be explained in terms of a theoretical phrase;
rather, it must be understood through analyzing the historical experience of the national movement in each
country: when Lenin advanced the right of national self-
determination, it was for the purpose of utilizing the
struggle against national oppression for the higher purpose of an anti-imperial war. Marxists have never regarded the demand for the right to national self-determination as an invariable thing; generally, it has been
regarded as a factor in the struggle for democracy and
socialism. Indeed, there are two ways of understanding
national self-determination — either as freedom to separate or as freedom to unite. Under certain conditions,
separation is appropriate and must be advocated. For
instance, the so-called "heroes" — i.e., the opportunists
— of the Second International, ignoring the fact that the
nations of eastern Europe were undergoing their initial
encounter with the oppression of the imperialists, still,
in these circumstances, opposed separation as a means of
responding to the imperialists' policy of annexation. On
this occasion, it was Lenin who stood out as an advocate

of separatism.[19] Again, following the success of the October revolution, Stalin, during the life-and-death struggle taking place in 1920 between imperialism and the political power of the Soviets, stated that "any demand for the separation of frontier territories would be extremely counterrevolutionary at the present stage of the revolution." Moreover, Marxists insist that unity is a principle closely related to the right of national self-determination. In his work on "The Socialist Revolution and the Right of Nations to Self-Determination,"[20] Lenin said: "The meaning of the right of national self-determination is, in political terms, simply the right of independence, of political freedom; thus, the right to cast off national oppression . . . , but this demand certainly need not be equated with a call for separation, and the breaking off and separate establishment of small nation states. It is simply a practical manifestation of profound opposition to national oppression of all kinds." Lenin also said: We advocate the right to national self-determination "not for the purpose of 'introducing' separation, but in order to promote and hasten the coalescing and harmonizing of nationalities in a democratic manner" ("A Caricature of Marxism and 'Imperialist Economism' ").[20]

In sum, the principal aim of Marxist-Leninists in insisting on the necessity of recognizing the right of national self-determination is that of opposing imperialism by seeking to make allies of the oppressed nationalities in the socialist revolution of the international prole-

[19] See Chapter Four, note 1.
[20] Articles written by Lenin in 1916.

tariat; it is clearly not their aim to advocate indiscriminately the separation of each nation nor to urge the establishment of a great number of small nation-states. On the contrary, while supporting the right to national self-determination, Marxist-Leninists have constantly stressed the question of whether or not a particular nationality, depending on the actual circumstances of time and place and the interests of the revolution, ought to be separate: only then can the question of its independence be decided. It remains for us to recognize that the historical conditions, which continue to be felt today, bearing on the resolution of the national question in our country are different from those of Russia and the states of East Europe at a comparable period. Because the Czarist system was not only a prison for the various nationalities of Russia but also the reason for Russia's being an imperialist country, the antagonism and enmity among the nationalities was very severe. Following the October revolution, therefore, certain nations, like Finland, broke away and, taking a path different from that of the Soviet Union, established capitalist states. Given these conditions, the Soviet Union favored the principle of national self-determination and permitted them to detach themselves, for to have restrained such peoples within a unified country would have hindered the people of these national minorities from having faith in the Communist Party. As a result of this action, the anxieties of these peoples and other minorities vis-à-vis the Communist Party and government of the Soviet Union were dispelled and, further, the unity of all the nationalities of the Soviet Union was strengthened. From this it can be seen that the Soviet Union, while actually supporting national self-determination and permitting separation, was still mainly concerned with strengthening nationalities unity.

Before Liberation, China not only had a long history as a unified state but was also, for a long time, in the position of a semicolony. Thus, as we have already explained, there was a long period, naturally, under a system of inequality among the nationalities, but all joined together in resisting the enemy, the imperialists, so that during a long period, also, the nationalities of our country were united together. It must be realized, moreover, that the different nationalities of our country had long been in contact with one another (in the case of Han contact with minority areas — for several hundred to a thousand years or more) and that this had become an established historical pattern. This involved the intermingling of peoples, especially as between the Han people, with its large population, and the national minorities with their vast areas; a characteristic feature of this process was the outward movement of Han working people. For instance, in Inner Mongolia, where Mongol people are concentrated, the majority of the population in certain areas was Han, and in some places Mongols comprised only 20 per cent of the population. Different peoples were mixed together to an even greater degree in other national minority areas: the areas in which the Hui were concentrated were extremely scattered; for the most part they lived in a dispersed pattern in Han areas. Even more pronounced was the situation of the Manchus. Only in the case of the national minorities of Sinkiang and

Tibet [and Outer Mongolia] was there a high, virtually complete degree of concentration.[21] But in political, social, economic, cultural, and other respects, these peoples, like the other national minorities, were ill prepared for separation; all the national minorities (including those of Sinkiang and Tibet), because of cultural and historical conditions, and especially because of close economic relations, formed with the Han a single, unbreakable unit. In recent history, certain national minorities in our country have experienced independence movements. Not only did these meet with complete failure, but before one foot could get picked up to walk away from the motherland, the other foot had already sunk in the trap set by the imperialists. This historical lesson has served as a warning for the leading personalities of China's comparatively large national minorities. Assuming that they did become separate without falling into the arms of the imperialists and that their "independence" followed its own course, the situation of such national minorities would simply have been that, having missed the benefits of the victory of China's revolution, including the fraternal, progressive help of the Han people, their difficulties and suffering would only have been made more acute. Therefore, the description, offered in the past by

21 Which is the very reason, as suggested in the Introduction, that the concept of a federal China, as put forth by the CCP prior to Mao's attainment of leadership, made such good sense. Giving equal weight to the interests of the Tibetans, Mongols, and "Turki," it was the obvious solution, but before the Long March had been completed, Han interests had been given precedence over the interests of all other nationalities in China. The national minorities other than those in Tibet, Sinkiang, and Outer Mongolia were no longer highly concentrated precisely on account of Han imperialism.

some people, of the relations between the minority peoples and the Han during the period of reactionary rule as "can't be seen," "can't break away" is an inadequate assessment of the concrete situation of the time in question. The "can't be seen" applied only to the reactionary Han ruling class, for whom the Han people at large were also "invisible." Today they have already been overthrown. The "can't break away" had to do with the people of different nationalities, and from now on they will even be drawing closer together. The Han people have the responsibility of assisting each of the fraternal nationalities, while the national minorities, for their part, must overcome the remnants of local nationalism as well as any feelings of solitariness, exclusiveness, and aimless xenophobia, all of which are harmful to nationalities unity and contrary to the interests of the nationalities. Since the reactionary Han rulers not only oppressed the people of each national minority within China but also oppressed the working people within the Han nation, the interests of the people of the national minorities and of the Han people are identical.[22]

The Chinese Communist Party, the deliverers of all of China's peoples and the leader of the Chinese revolution, was, of course, principally a product of the Han people. This was because the Han people had in fact

[22] To appreciate how extreme this position is, it may be remarked that Mao himself (*Jen-min jih-pao*, 8 August 1963) has analyzed the Negro problem in the United States in the same terms: viz., it is not a racial question at all but rather a class question, with the workingmen, black and white, united together against the cruel capitalists. Actual developments in China have shown the degree to which the Party's analysis is divorced from reality.

become, during the development of our country's nationalities over a long period of time, the principal people of China, representing more than 90 per cent of the total population of the country and, on the whole, leading the national minorities in military, political, economic, and cultural development as well as in other respects; in improving the livelihood of the whole country, too, the Han people were the most important force. Nevertheless, advanced persons and revolutionaries among the national minorities made a glorious and irrefutable contribution to the Chinese people's democratic revolution. No one can dispute that on innumerable occasions their precious blood and sweat flowed together with the precious blood and sweat of the Han people. Not only those peoples — such as the Hui and the Manchus — who live scattered among the Han, but other national minorities — such as the Mongols, the Chuang, and others — acted in this manner. During the second domestic revolutionary war, the Chuang people of Kwangsi, under the leadership of the martyr Wei-pa-ch'ün[23] and others, and together with the people of the Han nationality, launched an uprising on the Tso and Yu Rivers, creating a revolutionary base and the Seventh Workers' and Peasants' Red Army. The revolutionary force thereby established by the brave sons and daughters of the Han and Chuang people subsequently joined the main force

[23] This is known as the Pai-se uprising, which occurred in 1929. Wei-pa-ch'ün has become one of the foremost revolutionary heroes from among the national minorities. His life is reviewed in *Min-tsu t'uan-chieh* (Nationalities unity), No. 10 (1962), p. 24. Cf. Han Li, "The People's Liberation Army is the Brother in Arms of All Nationalities," *Min-tsu t'uan-chieh*, No. 8 (1959), p. 3.

of the Red Army and took part in the 25,000-*li* Long March. This revolutionary base thereafter experienced the utmost severity of the white terror, and the revolution passed through its period of utmost difficulty; revolutionary activity was discontinued. During the War of Liberation, a force of revolutionary partisans was again established in the enemy's rear, and it stubbornly persisted right down to the joint liberation of Kwangsi by a large army from outside and the partisans. During the Anti-Japanese War and the War of Liberation, the Mongol people, under the leadership of Ulanfu and other comrades, made a great contribution toward supporting the Chinese revolution. The national minorities of Sinkiang, especially the Uighurs, made a superlative contribution to the revolution by establishing a revolutionary base and accomplishing by peaceful means the speedy liberation of all Sinkiang.[24] The Li and Miao people of Hainan, together with the Han, under the leadership of the Chinese Communist Party, kept up an armed struggle for more than twenty years; they maintained a sizable army right down to the victory won jointly with the Liberation Army from the mainland. When the Red Army passed through national minority areas in western Hunan, Yunnan, Kweichow, and other places, these national minorities (such as the Miao, Yi, etc.) not only assisted the Red Army but also enthusiastically sent their sons to join, thus enlarging the Red Army's forces. Prior to Liberation, moreover, they energetically launched a guerrilla war which, in conjunction

---

[24] The minorities of Sinkiang sought independence, not "liberation"; the Mongol contribution to the Chinese revolution was minimal.

with the action of the Liberation Army, prepared the way for Liberation. As everyone knows, during the Red Army's difficult crossing of Snow Mountain and the grasslands, the advanced units were able, by virtue of the sympathy and aid of the local people of the Tibetan and Yi nationalities, to emerge victorious in this crisis.[25] The unusually vivid imprint of the contribution made by these national minority people to China's revolution must be given special and generous treatment in the history of the Chinese people's revolution. And so we say that "The history of the Chinese revolution is the history of the heroic struggle of the people of all nationalities led by the Chinese Communist Party." This is in complete agreement with the historical facts of the Chinese revolution.

*What was it that caused all of China's national minority peoples to join in the revolutionary fervor? It was their realization that a victory of the Chinese people's revolution would be a victory for the people of each of the national minorities; that independence for each of China's national minorities was conditional upon independence for all China's peoples; that only by forging a unity among themselves could all the peoples of China attain liberation; and that by proceeding separately they could only expect to meet destruction at the hands of the*

[25] According to Mao's own account, however, the ferocity of the local people — and the Tibetans in particular — was one of the principal hazards of the Long March. (Snow, *Red Star Over China*, pp. 180, 195, 204–205.) Clearly, their reception was a mixed one: while the Red Army was in general successful in gaining the neutrality, if not the support, of the minority peoples encountered on the Long March, this success was not uniform.

*imperialists.* Each of the national minority peoples recognized that after Liberation, as well as during the liberation movement, the assistance extended by the Han people for the development of the national minorities would be of decisive significance. Without help from the Han people, some of the national minority areas would not be able to establish an industrial base within a short period of time; highways, railroads, and other main arteries of communication linking them together could not have appeared quickly; and sizable amounts of modern industry could not have been established in a brief interval. These things provide excellent proof of the advantages of creating "a great family of all the nationalities." The foregoing clearly shows that: there are similarities between the national question in our country and in the Soviet Union; our development of a policy on the national question was in conformity with Marxist-Leninist principles and actually paralleled Soviet policy. This is one side of the matter. On the other side is the fact that, because the historical situations in our country and in the Soviet Union were not the same during the corresponding period — "the difference [being that]," in Lenin's words, "between an oppressed nation and an oppressor nation" — there were naturally differences between the national questions in our country and in the Soviet Union: consequently, the form and manner in which we came to a determination of the national question were not the same as in the Soviet Union. Although, for the above-mentioned causes, we did not emphasize "national self-determination," but only emphasized national regional autonomy, we still endorsed and honored this principle, and in proposing "regional autonomy" we were holding to the principle of national self-determination, and we followed the spirit of this principle in resolving the question. In resolving the national question, the Soviet Union adopted "national self-determination" and in due course implemented federalism; in principle, we followed the same course as the Soviet Union, but with respect to areas in which national minorities are concentrated, we preferred not to use the federal idea but instead put into practice the method of national regional autonomy. At the present time, with the oppressed nationalities having united together and opposed imperialism, all the nationalities now comprise together one big family that is progressive inasmuch as it protects the motherland and furthers lasting world peace, and even more because it promotes the political, economic, and cultural development of each of the nationalities and furthers their advance on the road to socialism. Why do we merely call this policy "regional autonomy of nations" rather than "national autonomy"? "National autonomy" applies to the collective exercise of autonomy by a single nationality living in different places in a particular state.[26] This is impracticable; it is a delusion of the petty bourgeoisie. It is therefore wrong.

26 "National autonomy" was the program of the Austrian Social Democrats during the period of the Second International (1889–1914).

# CHAPTER THREE

Safeguard the Policy
of Regional Autonomy That Permits
the National Minorities
To Be Masters in Their Own Homes

*National regional autonomy is the practical result of the
Chinese Communist Party's application of Marxist-
Leninist theory on the national question to the facts of
the Chinese revolution, and it expresses the basic policy
for resolving the national question in our country.* This
is the one key for resolving the national question, for the
claim to political authority (management of their own
internal affairs by the people of the national minorities)
is the claim of the united masses of the people of each
nationality. The facts of the Chinese revolution clearly
show that this policy fully reconciles the actual position
of the national question in China with the collective
wishes of all the nationalities: this is completely true.
Under the conditions of the transition to socialism now
prevailing in our country, to carry out this policy is to
reconcile completely the principles of socialist democracy and nationalities equality. Furthermore, in the carrying out of this policy will be realized the rights of the

national minorities to be masters in their own homes in accordance with the particular circumstances and special characteristics that have shaped each of them. It will also make possible, on the foundation of complete equality, the strengthening of nationalities unity as well as the collective management and building up of our country, thereby further facilitating the development of the nationalities by their own efforts. The realization of this policy is a requirement for all the people of the whole country. This policy of national regional autonomy has been energetically implemented in national minority areas since the liberation of the whole country. Already, twenty-seven national minority peoples in areas where they are concentrated in various parts of the country have established seventy-four national autonomous areas at the *hsien* level or above (including forty-three autonomous *hsien*, twenty-seven autonomous *chou*, and two autonomous regions [*ch'ü*]). They will be able to help the other national minority areas in carrying out the policy of regional autonomy by 1957 or 1958.[1]

All national regional autonomous areas are parts of the Chinese People's Republic and cannot be separated from it; national regional autonomy is a local autonomy exercised under the unified leadership of the central

1 By 1958 the devising of regional autonomy had basically been completed. In 1962 there were fifty-six autonomous *hsien* (counties), twenty-eight autonomous *chou* (prefectures; the *chou* is the next larger administrative unit above the *hsien*), and four autonomous regions (*ch'ü*, equivalent to a province). These last were the Inner Mongolia, Sinkiang Uighur, Kwangsi Chuang, and Ninghsia Hui Autonomous Regions; the long-projected Tibet Autonomous Region was formally established on 1 September 1965.

people's government, and the organs of nationalities autonomy have the status of local government, depending on superior, national organs for leadership. This provides protection for the areas where the national minorities live together and fully manifests their right to be "masters in their own homes"[2] (the right to establish their residence and to manage their own affairs). The organs of self-government in national autonomous areas not only exercise the functions of a local element, identical with others, in the national administration but may also, under the authority granted by law and the Constitution: regulate the local budget; establish, in accordance with the military law of the land, local security forces; and formulate autonomous regulations and independent laws that take into account the political, economic, and cultural peculiarities of the local people. The form of the organs of national autonomy can be determined in accordance with the real desires of the majority of the population in the area in which regional autonomy is to be practiced. In carrying out their functions, the organs of self-government should employ the spoken and written language in common use among the people of the area. As a result of carrying out the policy of regional autonomy, the organs of self-government of each of the nationalities have already instilled among the people of the nationalities of the respective areas a great enthusiasm for the exercise of political power; developed more intimate relations between the Chinese Communist Party and organs

---

[2] "Tang-chia tso-chu" — I have preferred a literal translation. The phrase could also be rendered, "manage their own affairs."

of state power, on the one hand, and the national minorities, on the other; aroused among the national minorities an independent spirit and a positive attitude with respect to managing their local affairs; strengthened the internal unity of each nationality; raised the patriotic ardor among the people of all nationalities; and set about promoting the development of each national minority with respect to all aspects of their life, including their political, economic, and cultural affairs.

The reactionary rulers of the past never allowed the nationalities within the country to establish their own political power in this way, but our state assists them in carrying out regional antonomy — that is, in letting them be "masters in their own homes." This contrast is further evidence of our complete sincerity toward the national minorities which, naturally, makes possible a spirit of mutual help among all the nationalities and provides a basis for cooperative effort. Only in this way can the relations and bonds between the center and the peoples of the frontier be made secure and mutual trust be established among all the nationalities. Only in this way, moreover, adapting the special features of the actual modes of production of the nationalities, and without infringing upon any of the rights of the national minorities actually dwelling together, can the backward nationalities be made to draw steadily nearer to the level of the advanced nationalities, and all the nationalities then be led together in the transition to socialist society. And only in this way can the education of the peoples of all of China's nationalities in internationalism and patriotism be strengthened, the tendency toward "nationalities divisiveness" be criticized and overcome, and the splitting schemes of the imperialists be struck down.

*National autonomous rights and nationalization*[3] *are the most essential and most central concerns of the system of national regional autonomy.* The right of the people of all of China's nationalities to management of their own internal affairs is clearly provided for in the Constitution: to interfere with this right would be a grave contravention of the Constitution. The people of all nationalities must be allowed to enjoy completely this necessary national right, and at the same time they must be helped in advancing the work of nationalization. Because national autonomous rights are the content of nationalization, nationalization is an aspect of national autonomous rights. In order to understand what national autonomous rights are, it must be understood at the same time what nationalization is, and once it is known what nationalization is, it will then, at the same time, be known what national autonomous rights are. We shall now examine this matter.

*What is nationalization?* Stalin has already, in terms of the national minorities in the Soviet Union, given an answer to this question. He said: "So that your people may be represented in all organizations, and your language and customs known, . . . autonomy means that

[3] "Min-tsu hua." The import of this expression is simply that local affairs in national minority areas should have an appropriately "national" aspect. There is a different term in Chinese to convey the idea of "nationalization" in the sense of bringing under state management.

you must learn to walk on your own feet. . . ." In other words, *carrying out the regional autonomy of nationalities requires that the national minorities learn to walk on their own feet in advancing toward socialist society: this is the national minorities' autonomous right.* To undertake this for them would not only risk making a mess of things but would also violate their autonomous rights. Therefore, cadres of the nationalities must be accorded rights and privileges commensurate with their position and duties — this is the essential meaning of nationalization. It should be recognized that nationalization may lead to divisiveness, but obivously this need not be so. Concerning representatives of the Chinese Communist Party in autonomous areas, it is simply a question of their providing steadfast leadership and correctly implanting this policy: then the masses of the national minorities can genuinely be won over. At present it is the task of Communist Party personnel to reduce the time required for them to learn how to walk on their own feet. Assistance in fostering nationalities cadres is therefore an urgent task for the Chinese Communist Party in its nationalities work. In order to win over the masses of the national minorities and to carry out the task of national regional autonomy properly, the ranks of the nationalities cadres should be strengthened to the point that it will be possible for the administration in all autonomous areas to be staffed entirely by persons of the national minority of the area. Only when all national autonomous organs are staffed by cadres of the nationalities, and they are assisted in their work to the point that they can assume responsibility, only then will a close relationship develop between the masses of the nationality and their organs of local self-government, the real situation be understood, and success be scored in comprehending the sentiments, emotions, and sufferings of the people of the nationalities. Han cadres cannot take the place of nationalities cadres in this kind of work. Only when Communism has become strong within the national minorities themselves can the Chinese Communist Party take root among them.

There exist among the national minorities representative persons and public leaders who have connections with the mass of the people and who are willing to serve their own people as nationalities cadres. The only question is whether we are skillful or not in using them.[4] In the course of the revolutionary struggle, and especially during the various struggles following Liberation, each of the nationalities produced a batch of cadres, and we were able to carry on with their development. Yet their cultural position at the beginning was not at all promising: the Chinese Communist Party has had this kind of successful experience. Indeed, a great many senior cadres of the national minorities were recruited and trained by the Chinese Communist Party during the long revolutionary struggle (many were completely illiterate shepherds). What it required was that we patiently train them over a long period of time, for which a train-

---

[4] This problem mirrors a whole series of difficulties between the CCP and the national minorities. The story is told of a Tibetan youth of noble birth who appeared for training at the National Minorities Institute in Peking — with his slaves as personal attendants. The slaves were given accommodations equal to those of their master and sent to school along with him for training as cadres.

ing system and plan were essential, beginning with learning how to read and write. Moreover, Han cadres were made responsible for patiently and ceaselessly leading their younger brothers in this work. Not only must we teach the nationalities cadres to be connected intimately with the people, but we must also encourage the nationalities cadres to love their own people and look after the actual interests and feelings of their own people, for these feelings are only what one would expect them to be. They must be encouraged to dare to reflect the actual situation and to risk putting forward unconventional ideas, for only in this way can the Chinese Communist Party and the national government take advantage of their ties with the masses of the national minorities and utilize the nationalities cadres as mirrors for the natural feelings and even the true situation of the nationalities, thereby improving our work. If we do not, therefore, "strengthen the man" by making him more responsive, he will not dare to express his own opinion.[5] The alternative is to allow nationalities cadres to acquire from Han cadres a tendency to become over-hurried and to ignore the natural feelings of people of the nationality in question. This would reduce the potential usefulness of the nationality cadres and finally lead to the casting off of the broad masses of the nation-

[5] The author is here referring to nationality cadres of humble origin rather than to those from a commanding social position. The former often tended to become too much identified with the Han Chinese and to lose thereby whatever chances they might have had of wielding real authority among their own people. The latter, on the other hand, tended to resist Han domination.

alities. This is not a profitable approach to nationalities work.

Both the Chinese Communist Party and the organs of Government have a serious regard for the work of fostering nationality cadres. During the past several years, the capital and the provinces together have founded seven institutes of nationalities,[6] together with a fairly large number of cadre schools and training classes, while special attention has been given to the recruitment and training of nationalities cadres in the course of our practical work. At the present time there are already 210,000 nationality cadres (of whom 80,000 are cadres of the Chinese Communist Party), a fact of the greatest significance for the development of nationalities work in national minority areas.[7]

*To take full advantage of the trust on the part of the people of the national minorities, we must not harbor "national secrets" vis-à-vis the national minorities but must, rather, let them apprise themselves about matters relating to their own people.* In the work of developing the national minority areas we must all not only let the nationalities cadres have the information they need but also clearly discuss everything with them. It is essential, moreover, to seek out and to grasp their views, develop

[6] These institutes were located at Peking, Wuhan, Lanchow, Chengtu, Kweiyang, Kunming, and Nanning. See Map 2. Other nationality institute branches have since been established, notably in Inner Mongolia, Sinkiang, and Tibet.

[7] By the end of 1958 the number of nationality cadres had more than doubled, to 480,000 (Hu Chun, "On the Training of Minority Cadres," *Min-tsu yen-chiu* [Nationalities research], [October 1959], pp. 19–26), but during the "great leap" years (1958 to 1960), the CCP was to discover how unreliable many of these cadres were.

a cohesive force among them, and to let them carry things out on their own. This is their right. If people of the national minorities are prevented from knowing about and taking decisions concerning important matters affecting their own people, or if it should happen that their participation is not welcomed in the management of such matters, this would be a violation of the autonomous rights of the national minorities which cannnot be allowed under the Constitution. Getting rid of "national secrets" requires, especially, getting rid of the so-called "barbarians are to be pacified" method used by China's feudal ruling groups of the past in dealing with the national minorities. "It is not our people whose heart needs cleansing": this wrong point of view handed down from the feudal rulers of the past must be thoroughly rooted out. We must have unlimited faith in the people of the national minorities. Nor, of course, should the national minorities guard "national secrets" from cadres of the Han people: they must be thoroughly made to understand that keeping "national secrets" from Han cadres and higher levels of the state administration is a disservice to people of the nationality themselves. But some of the alienation among the nationalities may continue to exist for a fairly long period of time. For this reason, the Han cadres must make of themselves models which the people of the national minorities can accept and in which they can have complete faith, for one cannot depend on administrative orders to resolve this psychological problem. In order to win their trust, then, one must first trust them, and this cannot be done without learning their language.

*Language is one of the most important attributes of a nation, and the use of its own spoken language (and the written language of those nationalities which possess one) is one of the rights of national regional autonomy.* The national minorities not only have the right to employ their own spoken languages, but they also have the duty to do everything possible to develop their spoken languages. Under the reactionary camp of the Kuomintang, the use of their own language by some national minorities, if not discontinued altogether, was vigorously opposed. Therefore, it is set forth in the Constitution of the Chinese People's Republic that "All nationalities are free to use and develop their own spoken and written languages"; and "In carrying out their functions, the organs of self-government of autonomous regions, autonomous *chou,* and autonomous *hsien* should use the spoken and written language or languages in general use among the people of the area." Again, in the "General Program of the People's Republic of China for the Implementation of Regional Autonomy for Nationalities" it is concretely stated: "The organs of self-government of all national autonomous regions should adopt the writing most commonly employed in its region as its main working tool, and when their work affects nationalities who use languages other than the one chosen, their written languages must then also be used." Since the lack of a written language, or the possession of only a backward one, is a hindrance to the development of a people, the state is steadily helping such nationalities in the devising of new, or the reforming of existing, written languages. In 1951, the former Government

Administrative Council, among several items relating to nationality affairs, published a resolution on "Assistance to nationalities lacking a written language to create one." Thereupon, the Linguistic Institute of the Chinese Academy of Sciences, together with the Central Institute of Nationalities and other bodies concerned with investigating national minority languages, carried through a number of projects, among which was help rendered to the Chuang and Miao peoples in devising written languages and to the T'ai people in reforming their language. At the opening of a conference on linguistics in December 1955 at Peking, the complete plans for nationalities language work during the next several years were brought forward. It was decided to complete, within two or three years and beginning in 1956, the planned work of investigating the spoken languages of the national minorities and of helping to devise writing schemes for those nationalities that needed either to create a written language or to transform one already in existence. As a result, more than six hundred national minority linguistic workers have already been formed into seven teams and are now at work in the national minority areas.[8]

8 By 1958 it was claimed that the government had helped three nationalities to reform their writing systems and ten others to develop new ones. These new systems are based on the Han-language phoneticization plan, which employs the Latin alphabet. At the same time, middle and elementary school materials were being published in a total of nineteen languages of the national minorities. (Chang Yang-wu, "Great Achievements in Nationalities Cultural and Educational Work," *Min-tsu yen-chiu* [October 1959], pp. 27–35.) For critical appraisals of this whole effort, see *China News Analysis* (Hong Kong), No. 234 (27 June 1958), and Henry G. Schwarz, "Communist Language Policies for China's

The following has occurred in some other areas: national minority cadres employing the local vernacular have been accused of "starting secret meetings" or of being backward. This is a serious infringement of the essential rights of the national minorities. As a matter of fact, the spoken language of the Han people is not the same in different places. As they were brought into closer contact with the development of communications, however, the Peking dialect gradually emerged as the standard and the northern dialect as the base. At the same time, the leading writers of modern *pai hua* standardized the colloquial language. Only with these developments, which covered a fairly long period of time, did a unified Han language begin to permeate the different regions of the country. The idea that it is useless to use the local language in national minority areas — the preference for the language of the master reflected in the expression "the guests usurp the host" — is not only a violation of the freedom of the national minorities but is also a futile way of behaving. Moreover, if we do not use the local language in work in the nationality areas, it will not be possible for us to get close to the masses; hence, we could not get a dialogue started with them. If it is thought that national minority languages which have not been fully developed can simply be done away with, such an idea does not fairly represent the point of view of the masses. We know that all languages have their inadequacies and that all must borrow foreign words. This enhances their value for the purpose

Ethnic Minorities: The First Decade," *The China Quarterly*, No. 12 (October–December 1962), pp. 170–182.

of discussion and vocal communication generally by adding new expressions and constantly enriching themselves. Naturally, the spoken and written languages of advanced nations are more complete and practical. Therefore, in order to facilitate the free circulation and study of new concepts among the nationalities and to assist the nationalities cadres in studying Marxism-Leninism and becoming familiar with industrial practices, we can encourage and help the people of all the national minorities, and especially the cadres, to study Han speech and writing.

*In executing the policy of regional autonomy, the form of the organs of self-government in all national minority areas may be determined on the basis of the desires of the great majority.* This freedom of choice is an autonomous right of each people with which others may not interfere. Attention must be given to the nature of the people in determining the structure and nomenclature (names having to do with the functions of the cadres): their old customs should not be opposed nor their taboos affronted. Take the term "chief," for instance. Among the Li people of Hainan, this expression has the meaning of "a [male] sexual organ" in the dialects spoken in Yueh-tung and Tung-fang *hsien*. If our comrades there use the term "chief" in referring to certain functions, especially if the chief is a female, the people simply laugh. It is said that the sound of many Han words, when translated into one or another of the national minority languages, is sufficient cause for a man to be cursed, so it behooves one to be careful. When our comrades have not paid sufficient respect to the nationality language while deciding upon an appropriate rendering for the perfectly clear term "chairman," the resulting translations have lent themselves to divergent interpretation by the local people, who have varied their methods of work accordingly. In other instances, as when determining the limits of fiscal authority, establishing a security force, and so forth, the meaning of the Constitution must always be adhered to. The designations pertaining to organs of self-government in national minority areas must be made to correspond to their true nature, which is that of a level of local political power. This local government should have an appropriate degree of authority with regard to local finances, without which its self-governing authority would be incomplete; it would then be unable to fulfill its obligations. Therefore, if there are empty names associated with regional autonomy, people will have the impression that "the national minorities are in their own homes but the Han people are the masters."

In view of the factors suggested already, we hold that nationalization and the right of national self-government are the most central and basic questions having to do with national regional autonomy. However, the requirement for being "masters in their own homes" and for "nationalization" must be harmonized with the general line[9] and main tasks of the Chinese Communist Party and the state in the transition period, with leadership

---

[9] "The general line for building socialism" is a phrase applied to the general ideological framework within which the building of socialism is to be accomplished. See Peter S. H. Tang, *Communist China Today: Domestic and Foreign Policies* (London, 1957), pp. 164–165.

from the center and from higher administrative echelons, with the leadership of the Chinese Communist Party, and with acceptance of help from the cadres and people of the Han nation. Since the actual situation of the national minorities is a product of the past, the assistance of the Han people and Han cadres is still needed for the reform of the societies and the development of the economies and culture of the national minorities; only with such help may speedy results be expected. If this pattern is not followed, then being "masters in their own homes" will lack substance, whereas by following this pattern the significance of being "masters in their own homes" will be enriched.[10]

*Where national minorities live in dispersed groups, or where a national minority is scattered amongst a larger nationality, conditions may not exist for carrying out national regional autonomy, but nationality* hsiang *[townships] should be established whenever appropriate.* The Constitution stipulates that "people's congresses of nationality *hsiang* may, within the limitations prescribed by law, adopt practical measures which befit the special characteristics of the people." In raising, on 29 December 1955, several questions concerning the establishment of nationality *hsiang*, the State Council resolved that:

10 Since 1949 there has been a steady influx of Han people into the national minority regions, where, on the average, the non-Han peoples were outnumbered by the Han even in 1949. The movement was accelerated during the years 1959–1960. In all, perhaps several million Han Chinese have thus migrated outward, enough to make a considerable impact on the frontier regions even if insignificant in terms of China's over-all population increase.

"All nationalities should have appropriate representation in the people's congresses of the nationality *hsiang* in which they reside." "Members of the national minorities constitute the main element in the people's councils of nationality *hsiang*." When exercising their functions, state administrative organs in nationality *hsiang* "employ the speech and writing of the local people" and "should take into account the peculiarities of the nationality in question." These decisions protect the political rights of all national minorities that live in dispersed communities.[11] For national minorities that live scattered among other peoples, it is required that they be accorded appropriate representation at each level of the state administration: this assures their inherent rights. They also must be helped to improve all aspects of their economy and culture. It is especially the Hui people, scattered [among the Han] in town and village, whose way of life and religion require protection and respect. Uniform and satisfactory arrangements also need to be made for the small merchants and traders in the towns and villages. Because it is especially easy for our nationalities policy to disregard people in areas such as these, we must in these places be especially on the lookout for and overcome great Hanism, proceed with the propagation of

[11] More than 1,000 nationality *hsiang* were established before it was realized, largely as the result of the collectivization of agriculture, that it was not practicable for these village-sized units to practice regional autonomy. They no longer exist as formal administrative units. See Hsien I-yuan, "Delineation of Administrative Regions of the People's Republic of China," *Acta Geographica Sinica* (Peking) (February 1958), pp. 84–97. Their situation was reviewed in an article in *Hsin-hua pan-yüeh k'an*, No. 104 (1957, no. 6), pp. 22–24.

our nationalities policy, and perform our nationalities work well. If our work in these areas is faulty, not only will nationalities unity be affected in these areas, but areas where national minorities are concentrated together will also be affected and they may not put their trust in the policy of the Chinese Communist Party.

# CHAPTER FOUR

# Help the National Minorities
# To Develop Steadily
# Their Economic and Cultural Affairs

*While implementing regional autonomy for national-ities, there is another important task to be performed: namely, that of helping the national minorities to develop steadily their economic and cultural affairs so as to improve their way of life.*

Why is this so?

This is because if the only practical issue of doing away with the system of nationalities oppression is a political, legal equality, this is not enough. If there are people who think this is sufficient, then they are, without realizing it, wallowing in the mire of opportunism of the Second International. These opportunists maintained that the important issue in the national question, that of national equality, was only a legal concept. This inter-pretation was firmly opposed by Lenin and the Com-munist International.[1] The latter recognized that on the

[1] For a cogent discussion, see Chapter II, "The Second Congress and the National Question," in Samad Shaheen, *The Communist (Bolshevik) Theory of National Self-Determination* (The Hague and Bandung, 1956).

basis of the right to national equality, real equality among nationalities must also be attained. For the masses of the national minorities, because of the limitations placed on their development, were made to suffer oppression, extortion, plundering, cheating, and unfair exchange at the hands of the imperialists and the reactionary rulers of both their own nationality and the big nationality; moreover, the extremity of these measures caused them to have a depressed or extremely low standard of living. Therefore, real inequality among the nationalities persisted. In order to eliminate this kind of actual inequality gradually, the economic and cultural affairs of the national minorities must be developed. As long as actual inequalities (including continuing differences in stage of development) persist, contradictions and even separatism among the nationalities will also persist.[2] This will not serve nationalities unity.

As we have already shown: "If the working class does not liberate all mankind, then it cannot itself be completely free." Thus, assisting the development of comparatively backward nationalities is not an accidental thing; even less is it a device to win over the upper-level personalities of the national minorities or to victimize particular people among the national minorities. Rather, it is the duty of the working class and the Han people,

2 As pointed out in the Introduction, this view has lately been discarded by the CCP, which has had to recognize that actual inequalities will persist for a very long time to come: development has now become *par excellence* the affair of each nationality, and it is class contradictions within the nationality rather than contradictions between nationalities that are to be looked for.

and it is of practical benefit to the national minorities as well as being advantageous to the Han people.

Although the elimination of actual inequalities releases the latent energy of each nationality (and this is very great), continuing help from the state is essential. The national minorities cannot rely solely on their own resources and energy.

In carrying forward socialist construction, therefore, the work of aiding the development of the national minorities is an important responsibility of the people of the whole country. In performing this task, moreover, there cannot be any discrimination or condescension in our behavior toward whatever nationality. Naturally, with regard to socialist construction, and especially the establishment of main economic and educational centers, state administrative organs must make rational plans according to the criteria of whether or not conditions are ripe in a particular nationality area for carrying out this kind of construction, the timing of the construction in the different areas, and the relative importance assigned to them. This certainly does not involve any inequality. It must be affirmed that all nationalities within the confines of China should have the opportunity, under the great force of state help, to carry out development in economic, cultural, and other fields in accordance with actual circumstances and conditions. Of that there cannot be the slightest question. And the state must energetically help each nationality not only in its political development but also in raising its economic and cultural level toward a position of equality. The state must give special attention to those nationalities whose economic and cultural development is comparatively backward and with respect to which the conditions for development are particularly difficult; it cannot limit its aid to those nationalities that possess large territories and disregard those with small territories, nor think only of the populous nationalities and not of the small ones, nor favor the advanced and ignore the backward; it cannot pay attention to those that live concentrated together at the expense of those that are scattered or live mixed with others; it cannot think only of those that, in terms of relationships among the nationalities, live apart, and not at all of those that are less alienated. The state must, furthermore, plan, continue, emphasize, and give special attention to promoting the establishment and expansion of industry in the national minority areas, thereby causing the working class in all national minority areas to expand steadily and become strong; thereby causing, too, all of the national minorities to evolve with sufficient rapidity into modern nations.

*The Chinese Communist Party and Government consistently take as one of their important responsibilities the giving of assistance to all the national minorities for their economic and cultural development.* During the several years since the establishment of the Chinese People's Republic, the state has already dispatched a great many cadres, a large proportion of whom were sent individually, to help the national minorities in their efforts to improve their economic, educational, and health facilities. This initiative has already achieved good results.

With respect to agriculture, a number of steps have

been taken to assist in the resolution of the difficulties facing the agricultural producer in the national minority areas. These include improved methods of cultivation, agricultural loans and production subsidies even more generous than in Han regions, and the distribution of modern implements. The utility of such measures for improving cultivation techniques and raising production is becoming apparent. In national minority areas where extremely backward methods of production were in use (some nationalities still used implements of wood or bamboo, or other crude tools), a variety of iron agricultural implements have been distributed free of charge. With the distribution of iron implements, the "slash and burn" method of cultivation prevalent in many areas was reformed. During the past several years the state has greatly aided the national minorities in building water conservation projects and expanding the irrigated area: in Sinkiang, between Liberation and 1953, the retained water was sufficient to irrigate more than 5.1 million *mou*[3] of agricultural land. The state also gives large-scale assistance to agricultural producers for overcoming various kinds of national disasters: according to incomplete statistics, Sinkiang's policy of producing for disaster relief had resulted in the distribution of 3.44 million *chin*[4] of relief food and more than 3.9 million *yüan*[5] of relief goods to help disaster-stricken people in solving their production and livelihood difficulties. But primarily it is in the agri-

[3] One acre equals 6.6 *mou*.
[4] A *chin* is equivalent to a little over one pound.
[5] A *yüan* is equivalent to a little over U.S. $0.40.

cultural areas inhabited by nearly thirty million people of the national minorities that there has been a tremendous enhancement of the agricultural peoples' positive production spirit, for here, in accordance with the wishes of the great majority of the people and the leading personalities having connections with the people, land reform and the consequent transformation of the old production relationships in the agricultural villages have been peacefully and firmly carried out. In these areas where agrarian reform has been completed, the high tide of socialist transformation in agriculture has risen up in the past few years, bringing about a decisive victory.[6] By the time the 1956 spring plowing began, by far

6 The "socialist reform" implemented by the Chinese Communists is supposed to have begun in 1949 (and even earlier in "liberated" areas) and to continue (virtually indefinitely) until Communism is attained. It consists of two parts: (1) "democratic reform" and (2) "socialist transformation." The stage during which "socialist transformation" takes place is often referred to as "the transition period" or "the transition to socialism." In economic terms, democratic reform means land reform (distribution to poor peasants and agricultural laborers of landowners' and rich peasants' lands), while socialist transformation means collectivization. Mutual aid teams are the prelude to collectivization, which is carried forward through the successive stages of cooperatives (lower and higher stage) and communes (launched only in 1958). The pattern has been similar in livestock areas. Cf. Chapter Six.

According to the Maoist formulation, "socialist reform" (commencing with "Liberation") is preceded by "New Democracy." During the "New Democratic" phase, all patriotic forces unite under the leadership of the Communist Party to oppose imperialism. See Mao Tse-tung, *On New Democracy* [1940] (Peking: Foreign Languages Press, 1954), and subsequent pronouncements, culminating in his 1955 report, "On Agricultural Cooperativization" (Peking: Foreign Languages Press, 1956), and his 1957 speech, "On the Correct Handling of Contradictions among the People," *Communist China, 1955–1959: Policy Documents with Analysis*, with a Foreword by Robert R. Bowie and John K. Fairbank (Cambridge, Massachusetts, 1962), pp. 273–294.

the greater part of these areas had basically undergone semisocialist or full-socialist cooperativization. In the Inner Mongolia autonomous area, the Kwangsi Chuang autonomous area, the Yenpien Korean autonomous area, the agricultural parts of Tsinghai Province, and other places, from 70 to 90 per cent or more of the agricultural households had already joined higher-stage agricultural producers' cooperatives; in the Hui people's autonomous area of Tach'ang, in Hopei Province, 91.6 per cent of the agricultural households of the *hsien* had joined higher-stage agricultural producers' cooperatives. In other areas such as the Sinkiang Uighur autonomous area, the Miao people's autonomous area in western Kwangsi, the Li and Miao peoples' autonomous area of Hainan, the parts of Kansu Province where national minorities practice agriculture, and in other regions, it is planned that socialist cooperativization can be basically realized between the end of 1956 and the spring of 1957. In the course of agricultural cooperativization, quite a few joint cooperatives were established which comprised two and sometimes several different nationalities. The establishment of these cooperatives furthered the development of close unity among all nationalities in the course of cooperativization. Agricultural production in national minority areas has increased, on the average, by 50 per cent compared with the peak pre-Liberation year.

With respect to animal husbandry, which occupies such an important position in the economy of the national minorities, the state has taken measures to protect and develop livestock, help the herders advance in safeguarding and enriching the grasslands, improve feeding methods, spread the use of improved seed, prevent and cure animal disease, struggle against natural disasters, put up hay, and help in many other ways; moreover, with the establishment of a trading network, mutual support is being developed among industry, agriculture, and animal husbandry, and this is rapidly promoting animal husbandry. The actual number of livestock in animal husbandry areas has increased, on an average, by nearly 50 per cent. Moreover, in national minority agricultural areas where conditions permit, as in certain livestock areas of the Inner Mongolia Autonomous Region and the Sinkiang Uighur Autonomous Region, the socialist transformation of the animal husbandry industry is proceeding gradually and firmly. Down to the end of March 1956, 72.7 per cent of the herding families in the Inner Mongolia Autonomous Region and 40 per cent of the herding families in the Sinkiang Uighur Autonomous Region had already been organized, and while most of these were still in mutual aid teams, the number of producers' cooperatives for the livestock industry in all areas had nevertheless surpassed 320. In addition, nearly 200 state livestock farms, and a number of joint public-private livestock farms being run on an experimental basis, had been established in different areas.[7]

With respect to forestry, the state has concerned itself with the prevention of forest fires, rational exploitation,

[7] Typical state livestock farms are run by Han Chinese employing modern techniques and machinery. "Joint public-private livestock farm" is a euphemism used to describe the situation of wealthy herd owners operating under state control.

the fostering of forestry workers and forestry experts from among the national minorities in the area, and the energetic promoting of afforestation. Forestry production in national minority areas has made marked advances during the past few years.

Before Liberation, virtually all of the national minority areas in our country lacked altogether, or had extremely little, industry. Since Liberation, industry in the national minority areas, with state support and the efforts of the local people, has developed measurably. Up to the present time, 423 modern plants have already been set up. The Sinkiang Uighur Autonomous Region has successively established plants for steel, automobile repair and assembly, textiles, hydroelectric power, cement, and flour, as well as a state petroleum enterprise and other modern industries. The value of industrial production in the region in 1955 was 34.8 times that of 1949, and this year's plan calls for a further increase of 28.02 per cent over 1955.[8] In the Inner Mongolia Autonomous Region there are more than 160 large and small industrial plants under local, state, or cooperative management. In addition, a huge state-managed steel complex is under construction [at Paot'ou]. The 1955 value of industrial production in the region showed an increase of 24.5 per cent compared with 1954. In Tibet, a plant for manufacturing vaccines has been set up, and a

[8] Sinkiang's industrialization depended on Soviet assistance on a scale that was not available to the rest of the country (except Manchuria). The extent to which the national minorities have been involved in the industrialization of the frontier regions is difficult to ascertain, but there is no doubt as to the predominance of Han Chinese workers in the major new industrial establishments.

hydroelectric station, a leather-processing industry, and ironworks are scheduled to be built.

With respect to communications and transportation, the greater part of the new highway construction throughout the country since Liberation has been located in the frontier regions of the motherland and in areas inhabited by national minorities, and in the national minority areas the amount of highway restored and improved far exceeds that newly built. The highway routes involving major engineering were, among others, the following:[9] Kangting-Tibet, Tsinghai-Tibet, Tsinghai-Sinkiang, Chengtu-Apa, Lanchow-Langmuszu, Kunming-Talo, Lhasa-Shigatse, Shigatse-Gyangtse, and Phari-Yatung. Concerning railroad development, the Tienshui-Lanchow, Chengtu-Chungking, and Paochi-Chengtu lines are already in service; now under construction are the Lanchow-Sinkiang Railroad, the Paot'ou-Lanchow Railroad, and the Sino-Soviet and Sino-Soviet-Mongol lines agreed upon in 1955 to run, respectively, via Lanchow-Urumchi-Alma Ata [a further extension of the Lanchow-Sinkiang Railroad] and from Chining to Ulan Bator.[10] All of these are of great benefit

9 See Map 2. I am grateful to Mr. G. W. Creighton of the Royal Geographical Society for assistance in locating Langmuszu. Note that the map does not indicate the existing rail and road network to which these new lines were added. Most spectacular of the many new transportation links built since 1956, when Chang was writing, is the Aksai Chin road from Western Sinkiang to Tibet.

10 The Trans-Mongolian Railroad linking Peking with the Trans-Siberian was opened to traffic in 1956. On the Trans-Sinkiang Railroad, Urumchi was reached in 1962, but the Urumchi-Alma Ata section has never been completed. See K. Pavlov, "China's Railroads," Institute for the Study of the USSR *Bulletin* (Munich), Vol. X, No. 9 (September 1963), pp. 17–28.

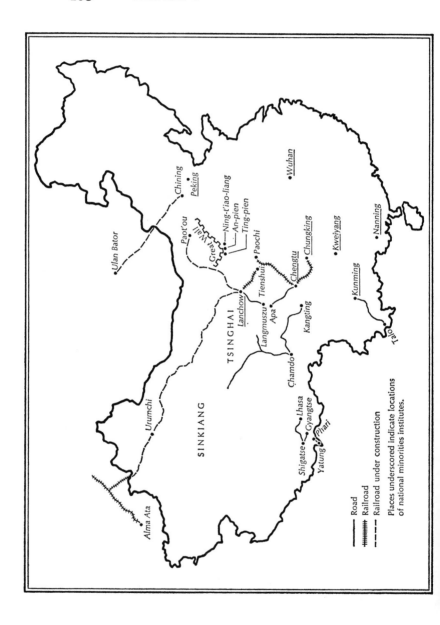

Ulan Bator

Chining
Peking

Paot'ou
Great Wall
Ning-t'iao-liang
An-pien
Ting-pien

Wuhan

Nanning

Kweiyang

Chungking
Chengtu
Paochi

Lanchow
Tienshui

Kunming

Apa
Kangting
Langmuszu

TSINGHAI

Tali

Chamdo

SINKIANG

Urumchi

Lhasa
Shigatse
Gyangtse
Yatung
Phari

Alma Ata

———— Road
╫╫╫╫╫ Railroad
– – – – Railroad under construction

Places underscored indicate locations
of national minorities institutes.

to the people of the national minorities in the northwest, southwest, Inner Mongolia, and elsewhere. Furthermore, test flights have already been successfully made on the Peking-Lhasa air route. Postal and telegraphic services have also been greatly developed in national minority areas.

Government-managed trade in the national minority areas is conscientiously looked after by the state. In the past few years a great many points for state trade have been established in national minority areas throughout the country: trade has developed in the farthest mountain districts and pastoral areas on the frontier. Fair and just standards of value are employed in the purchase of local produce and the sale of goods required by the local people for production or consumption.

During the past few years, too, educational and health facilities have expanded rapidly in national minority areas. The first primary school in Tibet was established only in 1952, but today there are already thirty-one; moreover, preparations have been made for the establishment of middle schools.[11] The Inner Mongolia and Sinkiang Uighur Autonomous Regions have not only expanded their professional training centers, but they are now getting ready to set up general universities. A great deal has also been done in socialist education and in the development of the national minorities' culture and arts. Many song and dance troupes of the nationalities, film projection teams, cultural houses, radio-listening places, and so forth, have been set up throughout the country.

[11] By the summer of 1965, Tibet could claim 1,600 primary schools and seven middle schools. (*New China News Agency*, 31 August 1965.)

The state has also brought together a large number of traditional stories and accounts of new events having to do with the national minorities, and many films have dubbed in the languages of the national minorities. With respect to publishing, in the one year 1955 there were published in languages of the national minorities 21 newspapers, 32 magazines, and 1,011 books, totaling 7,343,000 copies altogether.

With respect to health and medical work, down to the end of 1953, all the national minority areas together had 38 hospitals with 2,373 beds and 309 *hsien* health centers with 2,959 beds, plus a great many quarantine stations and maternity centers. In addition, many health teams dispatched by central and local authorities have brought medical care to national minority areas: serious and dangerous maladies such as venereal disease, malaria, and plague have been brought under control, and health conditions in the national minority areas have been radically transformed.[12]

As a result of these various kinds of development in areas that previously had no economic and cultural centers, such as the Hainan Li and Miao peoples' autonomous *chou*, the Kwangsi Miao people's autonomous *chou*, and other places, new cities and markets have now made their appearance.

The developments just described are steadily trans-

---

[12] It is claimed by the Chinese Communists that, owing to the rampancy of disease, the populations of the national minorities were steadily declining before 1949, and that this trend has since been reversed. See, for instance, Wang Feng, "The Great Victory in Our Nationalities Policy," *Jen-min jih-pao* (27 September 1959).

forming the mean and backward appearance that the national minorities of our country had inherited from the past; moreover, they provide an extremely good foundation for promoting unity and secure development.

During the transition period, the practical tasks of the Chinese Communist Party and State with respect to the national question are to open the way for each nationality to make the transition to socialist society, to expand assistance to the national minoriites in developing their political, economic, and cultural affairs, and to eliminate actual inequality. We must exert ourselves for a long time to come in order to make sure that these tasks are fulfilled.

# CHAPTER FIVE

Respect the Traditional Customs
and Religious Beliefs
of the National Minorities

*We must respect the traditional customs and religious
beliefs of the national minorities; the Chinese Communist Party and the Central People's Government insist
upon freedom of religion.* It is stipulated in our national Constitution: All citizens of the Chinese People's
Republic enjoy freedom of religion. Moreover, in their
actual work the Chinese Communist Party and the
Central People's Government guarantee that the people
of each nationality are able to enjoy freedom of religion
in practice. The Chinese Communist Party and the
Central People's Government have repeatedly declared
that this policy regarding religion will not change for a
long time to come. As long as there are still individuals
with religious faith among the people of China's nationalities, the Chinese Communist Party and Central
People's Government must honor and protect their
religious freedom. This policy is enthusiastically supported by all the nationalities.

In general, the national minorities in our country

follow a religion.[1] Buddhism and Islam have even spread to a number of national minorities and deeply influenced them, in many cases becoming the religion of almost the entire nationality. *Therefore, the religious question in national minority areas is closely connected with the national question and is an important element in it; it is, furthermore, a mass question.*

Communists are atheists and materialists; they do not believe in religion. However, Communists are historical materialists. They thoroughly understand the origin and development of religion and recognize the fact that, due to historical and social causes which still exist, present-day religions continue to have many adherents. It is clear to Communists that religion is produced from "a fear of spirits establishing itself in the mind" and from all that is incomprehensible to man. They recognize that religion cannot counteract natural and social forces and that help cannot be received by means of mystical revelations brought on by earnest praying. Thus, from its origins in the superstitions of primeval society, religion was developed into a system in the milieu of class societies in which, owing to its usefulness to the exploiting class, it attained its ultimate development. In old China before Liberation, imperialism and the Kuomintang reactionary clique sought in many ways to circumscribe religion and to turn it into a reliable instrument of control. To resolve the religious question, therefore, not only must classes be

1 And, in general, the Han Chinese do not — notwithstanding their ancestor cult — follow a religion. To a large extent, therefore, the freedom of religion has to do specifically with the national minorities.

completely done away with but we must also greatly
develop the means for controlling the forces of nature.
Thus, only through reliance on the development of
political, economic, cultural, and educational affairs,
and on the practical results of socialist reform — which
will naturally and indirectly extend the scope of the
struggle for socialism and spread the influence of materialism — can this question be resolved. All simple and
impatient methods are wrong; they will not suffice. In
his work, "The Attitude of the Workers' Party Toward
Religion,"[2] Lenin pointed out that ". . . this struggle
must be connected with the actual development of the
class movement which seeks to do away with the social
basis of religion." In the same work, Lenin dismissed
all schemes which sought to use atheistic propaganda to
"crush religion" as manifestations of "a culturalist
point of view which exhibits both superficiality and the
narrow-mindedness of the bourgeoisie." On the basis
of general Marxist-Leninist principles combined with
the actual facts of the Chinese revolution, the Chinese
Communist Party has not only taken a completely
solicitous and respectful attitude toward each of China's
religions and especially those of China's national minorities, but it has also, in the political field, chosen a policy
of cooperation with followers of religions. Since the
establishment of the People's Republic of China, the
Party has furthered in every way the anti-imperialist
and patriotic education of all religious circles, and
helped them to eliminate gradually the influence of imperialism and the Kuomintang reactionary clique and to
expose and clean up counterrevolutionary elements,

[2] An article written in 1909.

thereby purifying the religious circles, safeguarding the patriotic freedom of the great bulk of religious followers, and uniting with all patriotic religious personnages in the People's Democratic United Front.[3] Moreover, during socialist reform, religious functionaries must be adequately helped in resolving their problems of livelihood. In this way unity between religious people and nonreligious people is strengthened, as it is also within the religious circles themselves; as a consequence, unity among the nationalities can be further strengthened. To recapitulate what has been said, the religious question in the national minority regions of our country is intimately connected with the national question; it is also a mass question. This arises from the persecution of nationalities in the past, when the national minorities themselves were still not free concerning religion, and were discriminated against. Consequently, in their struggle against nationalities oppression, the national minorities often raised the banner of "protect religion," in which case religion provided the link for the unification of the nationality.[4] The respect we show for the religious beliefs of the national minorities serves

[3] Unlike China's united front of nationalities, which is the subject of Chapter Seven, the People's Democratic United Front has a formal structure in the CPPCC (Chinese People's Political Consultative Congress). The CCP seeks to group in the CPPCC religious leaders, leaders of democratic parties, and prominent non-Communists generally; representatives of the national minorities are included, too.

[4] This was particularly the case with the Hui (Chinese Moslems), whose great rebellions of the nineteenth and early twentieth centuries engulfed much of southwest and northwest China and contributed directly to the collapse of the Ch'ing dynasty. The designation of the Chinese Moslems — ethnically and linguistically Han Chinese — as a "national minority" by the Chinese Communists was clearly an effort to mollify the Hui.

the political unification of the nationalities. Otherwise, the religious sentiments of the national minorities may be repressed: this would serve the divisive schemes of the imperialist elements who wrap themselves in foreign religious clothes. This would not only be disadvantageous to the work of democratic reform and socialist reform among the national minorities but could also gravely harm nationalities unification. Islam, Buddhism, Catholicism, and Protestantism all have a great many adherents throughout the world; in Eastern countries it is especially Islam and Buddhism that have large followings. *To deal correctly with the internal religious problem will thus have a bearing upon the peaceful international relations of our country and be beneficial to the unity and cooperation of the forces for international peace.* The adoption of a simple, crude attitude toward these religions would have international repercussions, causing certain people to become more distrustful of our country and adversely affecting efforts toward peace. Therefore, the policy of freedom of religious belief is the fundamental policy of the Chinese Communist Party with respect to the religious question. A great deal of work is still required to make this policy truly effective. We must conscientiously protect the religious freedom of the masses; positively unite the senior religious figures; energetically foster patriotic, anti-imperialist, positive elements from among religious circles; universally advance the indoctrination of religious circles in patriotic and civic virtues; steadily restrict and repress the illegal activities of lawless elements from religious circles; and firmly bring under control the counterrevolutionary elements hidden within the religions. Only such a procedure will facilitate the enlistment of patriotic religious personages in the People's Demoncratic United Front and contribute to successful progress in the coordination of democratic reform and socialist construction.[5]

*Similarly, we must be cautious and respectful toward the traditional customs and habits of the national minorities, for they constitute an inseparable part of the national question.* The Constitution of our country declares that all nationalities are free to maintain or alter their own customs and habits. This principle is, furthermore, supported by the people of each nationality.

The traditional customs and habits of the national minorities can, for the most part, be divided into three categories. We should, in accordance with the spirit of the Constitution and on the basis of the free will of the masses of the national minorities, adopt different attitudes with respect to the three groups. (1) We should promote and make use of those which are favorable to development and production: for instance, boldness, martial spirit, fondness for work, sincerity, love of singing and dancing, free choice in marital matters, and so forth. Usages such as these are among the excellent traditions of the national minorities and ought to be publicized. But if some of these should tend to have an adverse effect upon the development of the livelihood

[5] In his 1962 article on the religious question, cited in the Introduction, Chang suggests that the religious beliefs of the national minorities may persist even after the establishment of Communism throughout the whole country. This is tantamount to saying that religion is permanent.

of the people in question, then they must be led to correct them. (2) As for those which are not injurious to, or which influence only slightly, the production and development of the nationality, or which may have had some influence on physical health but whose influence on present production is not too great, then their desires in the matter should be complied with or the right moment to advance their education awaited. These customs are mainly those connected with everyday life, for instance, branding the face, tattooing the body, mating festivals, and puberty rites.* (3) The national minorities must, as conditions permit, be taught constantly to abandon customs that are harmful to their development and to the present requirements of production. This is particularly so in the case of superstitious practices that involve human life, such as witch-vengeance, life-trading, and others.†

---

* The mating festival is a custom practiced by the Yao people of Lien-nan, Kwangtung. It takes place at the beginning of the first month of the lunar calendar. After a suitable piece of level ground has been chosen, the male and female youths are called to sing and dance with each other, the main point being to bring together forthwith the unmarried boys and girls by having them choose their mates, but at this time the married men and women usually mix in freely and permissively. Puberty rites among the Li people of Kwangtung and Hainan take the form of "enticement huts." When girls reach the age of thirteen or fourteen, their parents build a separate little house for them; living there, she meets with her lovers, and the parents of the girl seek more youths to send to her, thus enhancing her honor.

† Witch-vengeance is a form of "sorcery" that can, theoretically, seriously injure and even kill a person; actually, there is no such thing, for in practice it is simply a case of the accused person (sometimes a person taken by mistake) being beaten to death, buried alive, or hung by the people. Life-trading is another custom of the Yao people of Lien-nan, Kwangtung. If a feud develops between two houses, one or both sides

These customs and habits must be allowed to undergo gradual suppression, in appropriate ways, by the nationalities themselves. Impetuous and stern orders will not do; rather, constant persuasion must be employed. Once the sympathy of a majority of the common people has been obtained, then the matter can be looked to again. In particular, propaganda work should be avoided at first. Instead, the method of winning over the obdurate elements should be employed.

We need to emphasize Lenin's famous words: "A custom followed by a great many people is a fearsome force." We must be very careful in our approach to the customs and habits of each national minority, and recognize more fully that the reform of undesirable customs and habits requires a lengthy period of education. It is in the steady raising of the productive force and cultural level of the society that these questions can finally be resolved. This is because, with the development of production and the modernization of society, men are able to use their own resources to resolve their problems and difficulties, and it becomes natural for the masses

---

will frequently try to overcome the difficulty by forming a marriage bond. A feast is then held, at which time they reach a decision as to whether they should fight or let the matter drop. If they decide to fight, a date is fixed; when the time comes, both sides mobilize. If, on the other hand, they decide on peace, people from both sides are chosen to negotiate a settlement. Reaching an agreement is called "putting up the bridge," whereas failure to reach an agreement, when the participants have declared the negotiations abandoned, is called "tearing down the bridge." After "tearing down the bridge," it is not considered to be contrary to custom for the two sides simply to start killing. Therefore, the middlemen take advantage of the opportunity to extort money by threatening to declare a "tearing down the bridge."

gradually to stop putting their trust in these sorts of superstitions. At the same time, in differentiating among the customs of the national minorities, we cannot take the old habits and viewpoints of the Han people as a guide for our decisions. For example, a number of the national minorities have not regarded sex life as a serious matter: if we now take a hard line with their puberty rites and mating festivals, and do not wait for the appropriate time to carry out education, the result would be to alienate the great majority of the people of the national minority.

With respect to the undesirable customs and habits, it is necessary, on the basis of the free will of the masses, to adopt the method of reformist education through which they may be persuaded to give them up freely; in a great many cases, moreover, the use of roundabout means may greatly surpass the way of oppressive commands, which only too often leads to no good results, and under certain conditions it may be superior to the method of direct, positive propaganda.

# CHAPTER SIX

# Socialist Reform
# in the National Minority Areas

Why should socialist reform (including democratic reform and socialist transformation) be carried out in national minority areas? This is because the substitution of nationalities equality for the system of nationalities oppression will not, in itself, suffice to enable the people of the national minorities to do away thoroughly with actual inequality. *The only sure foundation for the complete equality of all nationalities is for each national minority, just as the Han nationality did (successively), to attain socialist society.* Lenin spoke with great penetration on this subject in his "First Draft on the National and Colonial Questions."[1] He said:

Underlying the whole policy of the Communist International on the national and colonial question is the need to make the proletariat and laboring masses of all nationalities and countries draw together in order to carry forward together the revolutionary struggle to overthow the landlord and capitalist

[1] "Preliminary Draft of Theses on the National and Colonial Questions" (for the Second Congress of the Communist International) (June 1920).

classes. Only with this kind of relationship can the victory over capitalism be assured, and without the defeat of capitalism it will not be possible to uproot completely nationalities oppression and nationalities inequality.

Furthermore, it is clear that on the national plane the solidarity of the motherland and the unity of all nationalities cannot be assured unless the transition to socialist society is made together; the complex of influences which this transition of all parts of the country together will bring to bear upon the national minorities will make it impossible for them to remain uninvolved. If the national minorities do not embark upon this transition to socialist society, then the whole country cannot completely attain socialism. And if national minorities within the country do not cross over, there will be no way, on the international plane, to win the sympathy and support of the oppressed nationalities of the colonies and semicolonies. Therefore, reform is of major importance, and the decision to undertake reform is basic. Except for individuals who may intend to oppress the people indefinitely, everyone will be ready to acquiesce in and support reform. The question, rather, is the method to be used in carrying out reform. *In view of actual conditions in China, with a united front between the laboring people and upper-level personalities an existing and developing fact, peaceful means must be adopted for carrying out the socialist transformation (and democratic reform in those areas where it has not yet been carried out) in national minority areas.* To adopt peaceful means is not, however, to deny the class struggle. Peaceful reform is a particular form of the class struggle; its aim, content, and nature are all, beyond question, revolutionary, but in terms of methodology it makes it possible for the national minority areas to choose workable means of proceeding that are congenial and indirect. This is to say that "reform" is a major, unalterable matter of principle. But as for the method of reform, there can be "flexibility within the principles."

*In taking this approach of truly peaceful reform, we must wholeheartedly respect the sensibilities of the national minority people and the peculiarities of nationality areas.* Thus, it is necessary for the people, according to their own wishes, to come to a decision on the timing for carrying out reform. If the time is still not ripe, then, while patiently educating the masses and elevating their sentiments, it must be awaited. When the opportunity does come, it must proceed at a pace and by methods determined by the national minority itself in view of its own characteristics. Han cadres should provide help, but they cannot put themselves in charge, and still less can they, in their work, mechanically adopt methods used in Han nationality areas.

It is no secret that the target of peaceful transformation is the exploiting class. But the situation must be clarified. The contradiction between a part of the exploiting elements — those who are at the same time national and religious upper-class elements — and the laboring people can be resolved only within the process of socialist reform. But the overwhelming majority of this group of upper-class figures all take a patriotic position, and due to their definite connections — based on nationality and also, in part, on religion — with the laboring people of the nationality in question they have become leaders of the people. We cannot view these persons in the same perspective as Han landlords. As long as they are not counterrevolutionaries, no simple disposition of their cases can be made. They cannot be rejected but must, rather, be negotiated with and brought into line by persuasion; they must be won over to an acceptance of the method of peaceful reform and their sympathy and participation secured. In our country at present, with the forces of socialism enjoying an absolute advantage, with socialist reform having become a great pushing force, and under the conditions of our joining with the upper-level personages of the national minorities in the united front, this is a feasible way of proceeding. Its advantages lie in lessening resistance and avoiding a further increase of national alienation and religious contentiousness. It also makes it possible to avoid a deterioration in production. Nor is this all, for on the positive side it promotes nationalities unity; serves to win over, for the benefit of society, the intellectual elements of the national minorities' upper strata; and helps to further the building of socialism. It can be seen that the work of peaceful reform is complex and troublesome; nor does it penetrate very deeply. But it must be recognized that to accept these inconveniences is to avoid greater difficulties, and that the very superficiality of the approach leads to a correct resolution of the problem. Subsequently, over an appropriately long period of time, the residual questions may be systematically dealt with. Otherwise, "by hastiness we shall miss the mark," and the result, on the contrary, will be only to extend even further the time required for a resolution of the problem.

*In simple terms, the method of peaceful transformation comprises two lines of approach: one is persuasive education carried on by means of repeated, serious discussions; presenting clear reasons; and setting an example. The other is that of buying off vis-à-vis the upper-level personages in which, both during and following reform, the state organs take the necessary measures to ensure not only that their positions of authority are left intact but also that their working offices are appropriately arranged and that their standard of living suffers no deterioration.*

In carrying forward the reform we must combine the two methods of from top to bottom and from bottom to top, persisting in the bottom to top policy of relying on the laboring people by mobilizing, organizing, and, where necessary, arming them; simultaneously, repeated, dynamic, and frank discussions must be held between representatives of the laboring people and upper-level personages. It is inadmissible to negotiate in name only while actually forcing them. The more fruitful these discussions, the more readily can the majority be won over and the minority isolated. And only when the great majority of them are truly in agreement can the reform proceed. To win over the great majority, moreover, it is necessary, at the time of the negotiations, to persuade the people of the importance of reaching suitable compromises with the upper-level personages. Such compromises include the following: (1) material compromise (for

instance, leaving some of their liquid capital intact);
(2) compromise with respect to the pace of change; (3)
methodological compromise. At the same time, the
upper-level personages must be helped, by means of
our instruction, to move closer to the laboring people.
Without mutual compromise, one cannot talk about
negotiation. Fruitful negotiations must depend on the
general handling of administrative and legal procedures.
If in the discussions we agree to proceed in a certain
way, we cannot then act differently. Where this does happen, the assent already won from the upper-level
personages may be cut short, and this could make it
possible for reactionary elements to swindle the laboring
masses of the national minority.

Because of the influence of the high tide of socialism
in China and the positive socialist spirit that is increasing
among the masses in the national minority areas, this
point must be thoroughly considered. In accordance with
this situation, and so that our work of reform may be
successful, a schedule can be made on the basis of the
situation of each nationality. To be taken into account
are the comparative backwardness of national minority
areas, the relative complexity of relations among the nationalities, the degree of influence with the masses still
enjoyed by upper-level personages, the relative dis-
similarity of the base for mass work as compared with
Han areas, and so on. Even more to be appreciated is
the fact that any shortcomings which may develop in
our work are difficult to correct and it will be even
harder to restore our influence and re-establish trust.
Therefore, we must still be careful to advance our work

in a sound manner, thoroughly carry out the work of investigation and analysis, and overcome bureaucratism and subjectivism in our style of leadership and methods of work; we must persevere in a way of work which is realistic.

At present, democratic reform and socialist transformation have already attained a decisive victory in most national minority regions. Among national minority regions where the work of reform has been carried out peacefully, so successful and healthy has it been in many areas that it has won the support of the great mass of the people of the nationality and the positive approval of some upper-level personages. It must be pointed out, however, that it is difficult to imagine socialist reform being realized without encountering any obstacles or any need to struggle. In individual national minority areas, it has happened that some ignorant people, under the instigation of counterrevolutionary elements, have adopted a course of action contrary to the will of the great majority of the people of the nationality in question and have opposed democratic reform and socialist transformation. The actual nature of this opposition is that of class struggle, not national struggle. This is because the aim of the struggle for democratic reform and socialist transformation is to liberate the great majority of the people of the national minorities from the old system of oppression and to develop their production and improve their standard of living. A great number of laboring people of the national minorities have taken part in this struggle, in which the land has been distributed to the numerous persons who were either landless or possessed very little land and to the slaves and serfs. In the present struggle, people of the Han nationality are not as they were in the national struggles of former periods of reactionary rule, when they plundered and seized land; now, on the contrary, they give every kind of support to the people of the national minorities. But the problem is not as simple as this, for this small number of blind, reactionary figures of the upper classes is making use of national and religious banners; posing as guardians of the nation and the religion, they have tricked a part of the masses. This activity, which is opposed to reform, has thus, to a certain extent, taken on a mass nature in some areas.[2] Winning over the masses thus becomes the central problem. In this connection, the People's Government, in discussions with the people and upper-level personages of the national minorities concerned, has already determined a method which can satisfy the demands for reforms voiced by the people of the locality, protect religion, and appropriately take into consideration the interests of the upper-level personages who have connections with the people. Basically, then, the problem has already been resolved. In summary, in carrying out peaceful reform in the national minority areas, it is absolutely impermissible to avoid performing difficult work and to sail only by a favorable wind. In the na-

[2] Indeed, there is no evidence of any real enthusiasm for reform among any of China's national minorities. According to the theory of the CCP's national minority policy, a natural community of interests was presumed to exist between the Han proletariat (workers and peasants) and the laboring masses of the national minorities: we now see that this is not necessarily the case.

tional minority areas we must energetically and thoroughly make known the policy of the Chinese Communist Party and State on the carrying out of peaceful transformation in national minority areas and strive to the utmost to perform our work well so that the people of each national minority, according to their own feelings and utilizing their own efforts, will be able to traverse their different paths of total socialist transformation and, along with the people of the Han nationality, (successively) enter socialist society.

# CHAPTER SEVEN

# The United Front of Nationalities in the Chinese Revolution

Like the People's Democratic United Front within the Han nationality, the united front of the different nationalities, with the Han nationality as its core, has steadily expanded and developed in the course of the Chinese revolution. As in the past, this united front still consists of two alliances.

*The first alliance is that between the Chinese working class and the laboring people of each national minority. This alliance is the foundation of China's revolutionary united front of all nationalities; on this foundation there exists the alliance between the laboring people of all of China's nationalities and the nonlaboring people among the national minorities.* There is still a larger or smaller group of these upper-level personages within each of China's national minorities, and between them and the laboring people there exists a relationship based on "early capitalist" or capitalist exploitation, or else they come from an exploiting class background or are intellectuals who represent the interests of that class. Class contradictions still exist between these upper-level per-

130

sonages and the laboring people of the nationality. These contradictions can be resolved only with democratic reform and socialist transformation, the elimination of every kind of exploitation, and the transition to socialism. But every aspect of development in the national minority regions is, generally speaking, different from that among the Han people: the consciousness of the masses is lower, resulting in a comparatively slow expansion of revolutionary strength among the great mass of the people; as already described, the alienation among China's nationalities, and especially between the Han nationality and the minorities, still persists; and the influence of religion among the masses of the national minorities is vastly deeper and more widespread than it is within the Han nationality. For these reasons, within each national minority the upper-level personages have definite connections — based on nationality and, in some cases, on religion as well — with the laboring people. They have long been the public leaders of their respective nationalities. In certain national minorities, people of this type have a great deal of influence and authority. The Chinese Communist Party has made a correct estimate of the influence and usefulness these upper-level personages can contribute to the resolution of the national question and the safeguarding of nationalities unity; it recognizes, moreover, that these circumstances are the product of a long history of national and religious oppression. Therefore, if we properly undertake the united-front task of uniting with the upper-level personages of each nationality, this may, under certain conditions, have an important bearing on the development and successful handling of our nationalities work and make a useful contribution to the strengthening of the working-class alliance of all nationalities. This kind of work is, consequently, both necessary and extremely important; it is a kind of work that must be done well in order for it to succeed. But is this really possible? It is, for most of these representatives of the upper strata possess a certain quantity of patriotic, anti-imperialist sentiment that, given the pace of developments throughout the country, is enough to draw them into the united front. Moreover, our united-front work among the national minorities is wider than that within the Han nationality. This content of the united front is very broad: on one plane, there are tribal headmen of primitive societies, slaveowners, feudal nobility, herd owners, and capitalists; on another plane, there are the upper-level wielders of authority, the religious upper class, lamas, living Buddhas, imams, scholars, intellectuals, and so forth. It is esential to build unity in this way. The practical test for the quality of the work performed in carrying out this method lies in whether or not it can avoid bringing on national and religious clashes and thus, in effect, avoid causing harm to the interests of the laboring people. It should be self-evident, therefore, that the united front with the upper-level personages among the national minorities is long-range; in our nationalities work, the laboring people of the national minorities must be persuaded to proceed in this way.

This correct policy for handling nationalities relations did not emerge recently; rather, it was proclaimed by the Chinese Communist Party as far back as the Anti-

Japanese War period. Under this policy, which included all leading individuals who had connections with the masses, the people of each nationality were given assistance on the basis of anti-Japanese nationalism. During the War of Liberation, too, it was on the basis of this policy that a united front was established with the popular leaders of a great many national minorities to oppose imperialism and the Kuomintang reactionary clique. With the liberation of the whole country and the establishment of the Chinese People's Republic, this anti-imperialist, patriotic united front was steadily expanded and developed. It was by applying this method, moreover, that the peaceful liberation of Tibet was secured.[1] It has also been used for establishing connections with the people of quite a number of national minorities with whom there existed in the past only weak connections or no connections at all. In addition, it has been used to strengthen the unity of all nationalities and to make more intimate the connections between the government and the national minority regions. In these various ways the popular leaders of many national minorities have become useful leaders and intermediaries. They themselves have, moreover, definitely received political instruction and have attained a new progressiveness.

[1] Nothing could more clearly demonstrate the purely tactical nature of the united front than the example of Tibet. Tibet's "peaceful liberation" was enshrined in a 1951 agreement between Lhasa and Peking in which the Tibetans were given a guarantee that reforms would be carried out solely on the initiative of the Tibetan government. Once installed on the plateau, however, the Chinese Communists imposed their "democratic reforms" on the Tibetans in 1959, following a serious uprising.

The lesson to be drawn from our actual experience in nationalities work during the past several years is that if, in carrying forward our work in a particular national minority area, we do not at the start do a good job of uniting with the popular leaders who have close connections with the ordinary people of the nationality in question, it will then be very difficult or impossible to settle the organization of society in that particular national minority area. Lenin put the matter thus: so far as it is possible to unite with them, we must form an alliance with all upper-class elements who are connected with the masses. With respect to the general situation of China's national minorities at present, if we fail to follow this method in some areas, it will not be possible for us to ensure the security and unity of the motherland; this way, then, could lead to a break in our connections with the national minorities, produce confusion, and make our task of building socialism more difficult. This would not be in the interest of the laboring people of the national minorities, nor would it be in the interest of the laboring people of the Han nationality. Therefore, *uniting with the upper-level elements among the national minorities who have definite connections with the masses has no objective other than that of serving the interests of the working class and the interests of the laboring people of each nationality.* This, then, within the framework of our nationalities work, is our position on steadily cementing a united front of upper-level personages. It is especially in national minority areas that we must uphold the doctrine of employing peaceful means in advancing the work of socialist transformation. It is there-

fore necessary for us to employ peaceful conciliation
with the upper-level personages, make use of the policy
of repentance, win the upper-level personages over to
an acceptance of reform, and use indoctrination to
promote transformation among them. All of this adds
to the content of united-front work.[2]

[2] The import of the author's remark here seems to be that the national minority problem can be neither apprehended nor approached by means of a crude class analysis. He concedes, in effect, that the national minorities have an inherent unity which has nothing to do with class.

# CHAPTER EIGHT

# Guard Against Big Nationalism and Local Nationalism, Especially Great Hanism

From the preceding discussion of the various kinds of work, it can be seen that, in general, there have been great accomplishments. And the accomplishments of this work concerning nationalities stem from (1) the great, correct guidance of the nationalities policy of the Central Committee of the Chinese Communist Party and Chairman Mao; (2) the support of the masses of the people of all of China's nationalities as well as of the People's Liberation Army; (3) the achievements of the work cadres (including Han cadres and national minority cadres) in the nationality regions. Working and living in the national minority regions is comparatively arduous, and at first nationalities work was unfamiliar to everyone. Most comrades were, nevertheless, able to succeed in their work. They carried out precisely the Chinese Communist Party's nationalities policy, attaining definite results; they completed the tasks assigned them by the Communist Party and Government and received a warm welcome from the national minorities.[1] In their work, too, they acquired a great deal of experience; moreover, they sincerely devoted themselves to national minority affairs. This illustrates the lofty attitude of Communists and all revolutionary workers and demonstrates the invincibility of the theoretical weapons of Marxism-Leninism. *But precisely because we are Marxists-Leninists, we have the courage to expose all shortcomings in our work. Among these, a serious shortcoming is the presence of great Hanism. It manifests itself chiefly among some cadres who do not respect the authority and views of national minority cadres, who do not positively and patiently help the national minorities to be masters in their own homes, and who endeavor to take over the work themselves.* Because increasing assistance of Han people and cadres in the national minority areas is indispensable, uninterrupted progress in the relations between the peoples of the Han nationality and the national minorities, and especially between Han and nationality cadres, is extremely significant. Thus, the conquering of great Hanism has a special significance, too.

As we have pointed out previously: the system of nationalities oppression was done away with following the

---

1 There have been at least isolated cases of the murder of Han cadres in national minority areas. The story is told of one national minority who cut off the feet of Han intruders, leaving the maimed persons beside the trail as a warning to others. Mu Fu-sheng, in *The Wilting of the Hundred Flowers* (New York, 1962), p. 128, reported that hundreds of Han Chinese cadres were killed by Yi people in Yunnan; the Party, he said, refused to take any reprisals but instead sent in still more cadres.

establishment of the Chinese People's Republic. This is not to say, however, that among some cadres and peoples there is no longer any big nationalism or local nationalism. In particular, remnants of the great Han nationalist way of thinking persist. Therefore, the Chinese Communist Party and Government administration are very much concerned with advancing the education of the cadres and masses in internationalism and patriotism and with the task of stubbornly exerting themselves in the long-range struggle against big nationalism and local nationalism, notably great Han nationalist thinking and its remnants.

## What is great Hanism?

When big nationalism appears among the Han people, it is known as great Hanism.[2] Great Hanist thinking is, then, a manifestation in terms of nationality relations of the reactionary ideology of the landlord and capitalist classes; it is thus a Kuomintang ideal. We recognize that this great Hanist thinking has had a long history, reaching its ultimate development under Chiang Kai-shek's reactionary governing clique. Therefore, great Hanist thinking is really the reactionary thought of Chiang Kai-shek. This ideology is as different from the ideology of the Chinese Communist Party and Chairman Mao as water is from fire; there is not the slightest con-

[2] *Ta Han-tsu chu-i* is generally translated as "great Han chauvinism," but this rendering seems to me to have an excessively sinister connotation. Local nationalism and Han nationalism (or "great Hanism") are merely opposite sides of the same coin, the coin itself representing an antipathy between the Han and non-Han peoples of China which has abundant historical justification.

nection between the two. So we oppose this way of speaking: "The big Hanism of the Kuomintang and our big Hanism are essentially different." We assert that this way of putting it is wrong. We admit only that great Hanism is a historical phenomenon. The great Hanist way of thought which, in varying degrees, persists among some Communist Party members, is a residue of reactionary ideology from the past and from the Kuomintang of the present era and is the result of infectious contact with this way of thinking over a long period of time. There are no roots of this kind of thinking in the Communist Party itself. We recognize, therefore, that there is no essential difference between great Hanist thinking and the ideology of the Kuomintang other than one of degree. To express the extreme difference briefly, the great Hanist thinking of the Kuomintang is conscious and systematic, whereas the great Hanist thinking that exists among some Communist Party members is blind and simply unconscious. In our management of the national question, we cannot equate with great Hanism an incorrect act or expression of a point of view that occurs by chance. Big Han nationalism is the systematic, historically constant, and pervasive use of the principle of great Hanism in the management of the nationalities problem. This is an absurd, backward principle. Not only has it been unequal to the task of ordering nationality relations, but through it, one's own self has been seen as great while other people have been made to look puny; it fails to discern the contribution made by the national minorities in Chinese history, nor does it recognize the increasing usefulness and the important position of the national minorities in the building of socialism. In general, it is a pattern of thought characteristic of the exploiting class that, in its position, viewpoint, and methods, is incompatible with the principles of Marxism-Leninism; the two are, indeed, completely opposed. This is where we draw the line between the great Hanism of the Kuomintang and ours.

Taking the country as a whole, great Hanism or the remnants of great Hanist thinking continue to exist almost everywhere. It still represents an important, dangerous tendency with respect to the national question at present. Among individuals of the Han nationality who are guilty of big Hanism, the number of those who are subjectively ready to accept the ideology of the feudal landlord and big capitalist classes, to follow the reactionary path of the Kuomintang clique, and consciously to be willing to turn themselves into big Han nationalists is, after all, extremely small. However, no clear distinction can be made between ways of thinking that are opposed to us and those that are simply remnants of old ways of thinking and acting, and the number of persons whose ideology has not been clearly reconstructed, or whose level or socialist consciousness is not very high, is quite large. In part they do not understand the policy of the Chinese Communist Party, yet think themselves right; this is fairly general. In some places the persistence of great Hanism and the dangerousness of its nature have been underestimated, with the result that work has been seriously affected.

*Manifestations of great Hanism*

1. These are manifestations of great Hanism: lack of warmth toward the masses of the minorities and remoteness from them, indifference to the sufferings endured by the national minority masses from oppressive rule, lack of interest in the rights of the national minorities; there are even individuals who are spiteful and practice discrimination, feeling that their own nationality is a grade higher; they retain notions of national superiority. Other manifestations of great Hanism are: the notion that the national minorities are by nature stolid and lacking in resolution; seeing only the backwardness and failing to discern the good qualities of the national minority peoples; lack of appreciation of the contribution that the national minorities have to make to development; even worse, not acknowledging the existence of the national minorities and denying that they constitute nationalities. In general, it is the absence of a spirit of equality toward the national minorities. This is characteristic of great Hanism. Everyone who holds these incorrect views does not recognize that China's history and culture are the outcome of the efforts of all of China's nationalities together, and that without this collective effort in the future, the work to establish socialism in our country will be at a great disadvantage. While the various nationalities are at present at different levels of development, it is not the case that all the national minorities are backward in every way. Every nationality has its strong points; the level of development of some nation-

alities is definitely not lower than that of the Han people, and in some respects they may be even more advanced than the Han. The Han people still must study the strong points of the national minorities. All those attached to great Hanist thinking are able to focus on only themselves, taking no notice of other people. They even go as far as taking the position that there is nothing splendid about working among the backward masses of the national minorities, and they omit from their work the important aspect of serving the people. They base this outlook on the notion that when insulted, discriminated against, exploited, and oppressed, the masses of the national minorities fail to show much public indignation or united purpose and appear not to have noticed. With this point of view, there is no intimacy in their relations with the masses of the national minorities. As a result, work in some nationality areas has suffered.

2. In evaluating the characteristics of the national minorities, not to proceed in terms of the actual situation of the national minorities but, rather, in a mechanical way by applying working experience from Han areas: this is very definitely not in accordance with the procedures of our nationalities policy. It is an adventuresome way of proceeding, which rudely interferes with the religious beliefs, customs and habits, and speech and writing of the national minorities. And sometimes it even turns good things into bad. Although the reform of the old system or the bad customs of a national minority may be essentially a good thing, it may be turned into a bad thing if serious attention has not been given

to preparing the masses of the national minority by raising their comprehension and if the nationality's leaders are not sympathetic. The "transition to socialism" is certainly a good thing in itself, but if the work as a whole is not made to conform with the Party's nationalities policy, or if the nationality cadres have not been included in carrying it out, or, even worse, if the true opinions of the national minority cadres have been rejected and the whole thing carried forward too hastily, this is enough to turn a good thing into a bad thing. The instructions of state administrative organs can be carried into effect only in a way that accords with the feelings of the people; instructions that must depend on force for their implementation are necessarily wrong. For example, relations of marriage in some national minority areas are similar to those in Han areas, but conditions are still not ripe for applying the marriage law: if it is sought, then, to institute the marriage law in an inflexible manner, we may encounter mass opposition and sow confusion and passivity. To take a more extreme example, an attempt to raise pigs in areas where the Hui people are concentrated would encounter mass dissatisfaction. In general, comrades of this kind do not comprehend that there are some things that done tomorrow will turn out well but if done yesterday or today will go sour; they do not understand that in some things uniformity cannot be sought forcibly.

There are sometimes direct connections between these mistaken tendencies and inflexible style of leadership of related leadership organs at a higher level. But if the leadership organs in the national minority areas are comparatively strong and really understand nation-alities policy, these mistakes can be avoided or at least mitigated.

3. Some do not respect the self-governing rights of the autonomous administrative organs in nationality regions, nor do they respect the right to national equality; they do not admit that the national minority cadres have rights and duties but, instead, seek to sub-stitute the ways of Han cadres. Inevitably, then, the re-lationships established in such areas are not as they should be and alienation becomes serious. With respect to cadre policy, they fail to give attention to and develop nationality cadres, believe that the nationality cadres have no culture, and say that training a nationality cadre is as difficult as "leading an ox up a tree." In the selection of members for the Chinese Communist Party from among the national minorities, they mechanically apply the eight conditions for Party membership which are standard, and then they go to the extreme of adding one of their own: they make it a condition for entering the Party that the national minority cadre renounce the customs and religion of his own nationality. They thereby turn the eight conditions into the nine condi-tions.[3] Some national minority cadres have been refused

[3] The eight conditions for CCP membership are not mentioned in either the 1945 or 1956 Party Constitutions. According to Peter S. H. Tang (*Communist China Today: Domestic and Foreign Policies* [London, 1957], p. 104), they are as follows:

1. Understand the nature of the Communist Party and the principles of Lenin and Stalin with regard to Party building.
2. Understand the ultimate aim of the Communist Party of China — the realization of Communism in China.

entry into the Communist Party organization because of their taste for wine; Moslem cadres have been rejected simply because they do not eat pork. The young people in some areas, because they gather happily together to sing rustic songs, are considered by the Youth League to have an "unorthodox" style of work and to be undesirous of development. These comrades of the Han nationality do not realize that the fostering of cadres, establishment of the Chinese Communist Party, and building of the Youth League among the national minorities are fundamental concerns in our nationalities work; otherwise we would have no roots at all. The national minorities are to make the transition to socialism, and while their own efforts must be relied upon, they should initially take advantage of the assistance proferred by the Han nationality. Therefore, in their work in national minority areas, and especially in the fostering of na-

3. Be determined to fight heroically all his life for Communism, never shrinking back, betraying the Party, retreating, or surrendering to the enemy.

4. Observe strictly the discipline of the Party and obey its unified leadership; take an active part in revolutionary work; resolutely carry out the policy and decisions of the Party and wage irreconcilable struggle against anything detrimental to the interests of the Party, whether inside or outside the Party.

5. Place the general interests of the masses of the people above his own interests.

6. Examine constantly, by means of criticism and self-criticism, the mistakes and defects of his work, and correct them.

7. Serve wholeheartedly the masses of the people, modestly listen to their opinions and demands, report these in due course to the Party, explain the policy of the Party to the masses, and lead them forward.

8. Make an energetic effort to study Marxism-Leninism and Mao Tse-tung's theory of the Chinese Revolution, in order to raise his own political and ideological level.

tional minority cadres, Han comrades must speedily and fully bring into realization the nationality's right to equality and autonomy and fully develop the nationality's energies. Trust them; bravely letting them take the lead, use and promote them; put their sense of independent responsibility to work; fully evaluate and make known their progress and accomplishments; and constantly help them to develop and more fully promote their utility.

4. The existence of bureaucratism within the leadership and lawless activities among the cadres in national minority areas inevitably have an influence on nationality relations and definitely have some connection with great Hanism. For lawlessness, as well as any discriminatory or insulting behavior vis-à-vis the national minorities, is contrary to the law. In the Soviet Union, wrongdoers who transgress the law by insulting the national minorities are very severely punished. During Lenin's lifetime, the Soviet Union not only strongly built up the law against insulting behavior toward the national minorities within the country but also forbade insults directed at small or weak nationalities outside the country. Take the following as an example. During the time of imperial Russia, if a Chinese merchant happened to die anywhere in the country, the corpse had to be salted and sent back to China. This struck the Russians of the time as extremely amusing, and when they saw a Chinese, the porters, with an attitude of obscene jesting, would ask: "Need any salt?" This was unbearable for the Chinese. But following the October Revolution, the Soviet regime decided that this practice

was an insulting offense and proceeded to set a punishment for it. In the past we Han people called the country's minorities by such names as "T'a-tzu" [Tartars], "Hui-tzu" [Mohammedans], "Miao-tzu," and so forth, all of which have a derogatory meaning.[4] To take another example, the eating of pork is forbidden among nationalities that are Islamic. In this they are expressing their own free will. But there were people among the Han nationality who purposelessly ridiculed them; they went so far as to trick them into eating pork and then — even more harmful — to pretend happily among themselves that they really did not know that this was an insulting or even that it was an illegal act. Following Liberation, and with the powerful spread of nationalities policy, these insulting ways of acting and speaking ceased. Their roots, however, have not yet been killed, and it is still necessary to carry on education by every means; this cannot be considered as a small matter that does not merit close attention. It is especially in connection with the investigation of cadres affiliated with economic organizations in the national minority areas that we must establish uniform rules; overcome the capitalistic, entrepreneurial ideas and behavior within such organizations; and thoroughly eliminate the obsolete thoughts and activities based on "national minorities are for Han people to live on." Not only must their

---

[4] The character for *tzu* has the primary meaning of "child," but may also mean "eggs" (as of insects or fish). It then has a derogatory connotation when applied to a group of people. This usage has been dropped. But the expressiveness of the Chinese language went beyond this — to the use, for instance, of the "dog" radical in the characters for the names of some national minorities; it has now been replaced by the "man" radical.

transactions be made fairly, but all actual inequalities must be eliminated from our financial, commercial, and monetary schemes designed to help the national minorities attain higher production.[5] Otherwise, the alienation of the nationalities may be further increased and nationalities unity adversely affected. Areas or organizations which fail to pay serious attention to this question at the same time disregard the wise principle of nationalities equality of the Chinese Communist Party and State and ignore the serious nature of the question of national rights. We take the position, therefore, that bureaucratism in the command structure of the nationalities work concerned, as well as illegal acts on the part of cadres in the national minority areas, all are definitely connected with Great Han nationalism.

These manifestations of Great Han nationalism have, on the whole, been basically exposed and corrected as a result of the investigation that has taken place into the implementation of nationalities policy throughout the country.[6] However, in some places and among some organizations these mistakes not only have not been satisfactorily overcome, but in recent years they have grown. Experience shows that wherever the investigation of the carrying out of nationalities policy has

[5] After 1949 all commercial activity between Han and non-Han areas was brought under state control. Presumably, many Han merchants who had engaged in this trade prior to 1949 continued to carry out their functions under the new regime. Much has been said in the Chinese Communist press about the better terms of trade now available to the national minorities.

[6] During 1956 a major investigation into the conduct of nationalities work was made; its chief objective was to expose great Hanism. This was to give way in 1957 to a campaign against local nationalism.

been comparatively conscientious, with the criticism of great Hanism in the affected places and organizations being comparatively stern, the attitude of the cadres to nationalities policy is comparatively correct and the work has improved proportionately. Where, on the other hand, the investigation of the administration of nationalities policy has not been conscientious and the criticism of big Hanism has not been very thorough, a passive attitude has developed, the effort to overcome big Hanism has received a setback, and there are still a great many of the old problems in our work. Thus, in areas of this kind and in the work of the organizations concerned, the mechanical adoption of working experience from Han areas, making the work everywhere the same, and the phenomenon of Han cadres trying to take over everything themselves are major problems which still need to be overcome. This experience is of value for the investigation work into the implementation of nationalities policy which is still to be carried out, and should be studied and made widely known.

*Why is it that these places and the organizations concerned have not conscientiously analyzed the conditions for the implementation of the nationalities policy and have not thoroughly criticized great Han nationalism?*
Because it has not been genuinely understood in the places and among the organizations concerned that great Hanism endangers our work, nor have they recognized that the direct and indirect consequences can wreck nationalities unity and damage the relationship between the Communist Party and the national minority masses;

they have not realized that great Hanism inevitably causes the working leadership to lose contact with reality and to become passive to such an extent as to make the cadres reckless or indifferent, resulting in work which is careless, oppressive, and, at the extreme, illegal. Thus, because of the absence of real understanding in the areas and among the organizations concerned of our objective in opposing big Han nationalism, they do not realize that once great Hanism has been overcome it will then be possible to make progress in the elimination of nationalities alienation and to strengthen further nationalities unity, make firmer the relationship between us and the national minority masses, and, at the same time, elevate the cadres' theoretical understanding, and direct the positive spirit of the cadres and the masses. With these developments, our work can be accelerated and improved.

Some people are afraid of this method. They feel that it may cause the Han cadres to be passive, affect their positive spirit, and result in leaving the Han cadres "bound hand and foot" in their work. We recognize that struggling with great Hanism is a matter that has a bearing upon whether or not socialist society can easily be established in our country and one that involves principles of Marxism-Leninism. This attitude of struggling with great Hanism cannot be compromised with, nor can the fact of the struggle itself be altered. So long as traces of great Hanism remain, we must steadfastly oppose it: we must loudly and angrily oppose it. We should not fear short-term passivity, for passivity may cause everyone to become frightened, thereby bringing about repentance on the part of the comrades who have been guilty of errors and leading them henceforth to act in accordance with the nationalities policy of the Chinese Communist Party. By such means can our work be propelled forward, thereby enhancing the positive spirit of the cadres.

As for fears lest Han cadres, following their study of nationalities policy, appear to be "bound hand and foot" in their work, such anxieties are unnecessary. We acknowledge that the study of nationalities policy will make Han cadres understand the desirability for care and caution in their work. But far from binding their hands and feet, it will, rather, equip them with ideological weapons. If it is a case of leaving them bound hand and foot, it will be their hand which offends our policy and their foot which provokes lawlessness that will be tied up. This is as it should be. If, as a result, they do not dare to work courageously, this would show that the policy had not been understood; it would certainly not demonstrate that there was anything wrong with the policy itself. Among them there may perhaps be a few individuals who selfishly calculate — and this is even worse — that they can, while making a pretense of accepting this, hide their mistakes and spread an atmosphere that leads to public resistance to the policy of the Chinese Communist Party and the law of the country. That is wrong and unwise, and cannot be allowed by the Chinese Communist Party and State. The only proper attitude is one which seeks in every positive way to improve our work. Naturally, this requirement implies a period of adjustment in our work.

*Local nationalism (or narrow nationalism) among the
people and the cadres of some nationalities also exists
to a serious extent. The so-called local nationalism is a
manifestation of localism within the context of the national question.* It is a lack of awareness of the important nature of the collectively established great family
of the motherland and of centralized, unified leadership. It fails to recognize that without the assistance
of the advanced Han nation, it would be impossible for
the national minorities speedily to develop their political
institutions, economic affairs, and cultural life and,
therefore, to alter their backwardness of the past and,
finally, to overcome their actual inequality; and that
an unwillingness to accomplish the necessary democratic reform and socialist reform, without which
it will not be possible for them to make the transition
to socialism together, may result from excessive stim-
ulation of specifically local feelings among the national minorities. Because local nationalists do not appreciate the importance of the help extended by the
Han cadres, they adopt an attitude of displeasure at
receiving Han cadres who come to work in nationality
areas. Generally speaking, it is a question of conserva-
tism, xenophobia, and "the self-importance of Yeh-
lang."[7] The existence of this kind of attitude [among
local nationalists] is contrary to the interests of their
own people and unfavorable in terms of the future de-

---

[7] "An envoy from the Han dynasty came to that place and was asked
by the local chieftain which state was the larger, Yeh-lang or Han."
*Mathews' Chinese-English Dictionary*, Revised American Edition (Cambridge, Massachusetts, 1960), p. 1094.

velopment of all of China's nationalities, and of their own nationality in particular. This hazardous tendency has largely been overcome during the past several years by means of education. But if we compare the tendency toward local nationalism with the tendency toward big Han nationalism, it becomes evident that it is the existence of the latter that remains the more dangerous at the present time.[8] *Both local nationalism and big Han nationalism are products of a long period of history. Local nationalism is a by-product of the national minorities' resistance to great Hanist oppression. Both of these tendencies must be opposed, but only where big Han nationalism has been energetically resisted and fundamentally overcome can the tendency toward local nationalism be satisfactorily overcome.* If the same force is used at the present time to combat big Han nationalism and local nationalism, that would represent a failure to distinguish between serious and light: this is actually the method of great Hanism itself and will have the effect of tolerating great Hanism. Some national minority cadres, furthermore, still have a "self-abasing" bent of mind because of the oppression and discrimination which they have long had to endure: if they have not yet fully raised their heads, it is necessary for us to give them energetic support. In dealing with local nationalism it is also necessary to distinguish manifestations of appropriate national sentiments among the cadres and people of the national minorities. In some places appropriate national sentiments among the nation-

8 Within less than a year of the time Chang was writing, the CCP was to take the opposite view of the one expressed here.

ality cadres has been taken as proof of an exaggerated localism: this is entirely improper. Responding to the call of the Central Committee of the Chinese Communist Party and Chairman Mao, some nationality cadres have, in a positive way, searched out and warned of conditions contrary to our nationalities policy and sharply criticized and demanded punishment for activities in the nationality areas that are an affront to the national minority and that obstruct the implementation of our policy. They have, moreover, positively brought forward their own views on how things should be managed. This springs from correct national sentiments; it is not some sort of local nationalism. Not only should we be circumspect in our attitude toward these correct sorts of national sentiments, but we should also foster them among the nationality cadres. For if a nationality cadre does not have this right kind of national feeling, the significance of working as a nationality cadre will be lost to him. Moreover, it cannot be expected that individuals of the national minority who have only recently joined the Communist Party and Youth League should already be complete internationalists (naturally, individuals with serious local nationalist thinking are not allowed to join the Communist Party). Some national minority cadres do not like to wear the dress or speak the language of their own nationalities. During the reforms of the customs and even religious beliefs of their own nationalities, such was their deficiency of national sentiment that they dissociated themselves from the mass of the people. Naturally, one cannot speak of such persons as having connections with the people or as reflecting the true situation of their own people. What is even worse is their bureaucratism: just like those Han cadres who are guilty of great Hanism, and behaving like their echo, in their work these nationality cadres guilty of bureaucratism employ forceful commands and provoke lawlessness. Thus falling under the influence of great Hanism, these cadres, although they have not yet changed their nationality, are in reality already exhibiting great Hanism. The key to all our work, therefore, lies in opposing great Hanism, and especially in first overcoming completely great Hanist thinking and its remnants among Han cadres in positions of leadership at the *hsien* level and above in national minority areas.[9]

*As we have said, great Han nationalism and local nationalism are both the result of long historical processes, and while the class basis which gives rise to them is now undergoing transformation and gradually disappearing, it must be reckoned that their modification will require a comparatively long period of time.* In opposing it, therefore, we must employ criticism and instruction: we must adopt the method of constant and long-lasting education. But inasmuch as the Han people are among the comparatively advanced nationalities, it must be made clear that if great Hanism is not brought under control, then local nationalism cannot be effectively overcome, and other work will be spoiled as well. So we must be rather strict with regard to the demands of Han cadres.

In opposing these errors, they must certainly be criti-

[9] It is not generally admitted that there are Han cadres in positions of leadership at the *hsien* level in national minority areas.

cized on the level of principle, but distinctions must be made when we come to dispose of them. A clear distinction must be made between the intentional and the accidental, between the purposeful offender and the blind ignoramus. Again, we must distinguish those errors that are especially serious and prominent from the ordinary ones, and differentiate between those individuals who are able to acknowledge their mistakes and decisively correct them, and those who, despite repeated instruction, do not overcome their resistance in a thoroughgoing way. It is necessary, furthermore, to take note of the difference with respect to the political influences generated by their mistakes. We should be lenient toward past mistakes and strict with future mistakes. Organizational sanctions and administrative measures should be used for those elements who stubbornly resist, who fail to be reformed by instruction, or who cause serious lawlessness, whereas the general run of cases can be handled through criticism on the ideological level. But this does not at all mean that individuals can be allowed to violate a principle of Marxism-Leninism: Communist Party members must be willing to follow the path and the principles of the Communist Party; there can be no compromise between these and individual Party members. The glory of the nationalities policy of the Chinese Communist Party and Comrade Mao Tse-tung definitely must illuminate every corner of the country.

In opposing these wrong tendencies, there must also be a proper division of labor among the leading personnel. Leadership cadres of the Han nationality should be given primary responsibility for opposing great Han-

ism and remnants of great Hanist thinking, while leadership cadres of the national minorities should be given
primary responsibility for opposing local nationalism.
Only thus can we avoid side effects and "by different
ways come to the same end."

Some people think that, if the national question is
as complex as this, while the prescriptions of our nationalities policy are comparatively narrow, they had better
stay away from nationalities work. They do not realize,
however, that the population of China's national minorities is so large, that they are spread over so vast an
area, and that they are often intermixed with the Han
nationality to such an extent, that all work has some
bearing on the national question. This is a practical
matter which does not allow us to avoid this kind of
work: even if you do not carry on nationalities work
directly, other work you do may violate our nationalities
policy. Wishful schemes to hide this reality are idealistic
[i.e., contrary to dialectical materialism]. The only way
is squarely to face this reality and expertly handle the
methodology of Comrade Mao Tse-tung — proceeding
from actuality, exercising caution, accumulating experience, and, when confronted by difficulties, seeking
guidance from higher leadership organs or contacting
organs responsible for nationality affairs. And, most
important, in major questions concerning nationalities
it is necessary, in accordance with a ruling of the
Central Committee, to make a report to and seek instruction from the Central Committee. As long as we
have a clear mind in our work, grasp the policy, proceed

from reality, take the mass line, and deal with problems according to the work methods and administrative procedures, this work will then be very easy to carry through to a successful conclusion. Stalin said that "the national question is the most dialectical of all problems" and is an important part of Marxism-Leninism. The precious experience of the victorious resolution of the national question in China by the Chinese Communist Party is a valuable addition to the treasure house of Marxist-Leninist theory. Therefore, research into the national question and the study of nationalities policy are not only helpful to particular cadres engaged in nationalities work but are also very beneficial to individuals engaged in the general study of the theoretical basis of Marxism-Leninism, and particularly to those studying its philosophy and policy. The nationalities policy of the Chinese Communist Party is a creation of the Central Committee led by Comrade Mao Tse-tung. The history of the Chinese revolution shows that in the control of policy at critical junctures Comrade Mao Tse-tung has always been on the correct side. Every member of the Chinese Communist Party, including revolutionary cadres working under the leadership of the Communist Party, must rally around the Chinese Communist Party and the banner of Comrade Mao Tse-tung, in the broad popular mass further by every means indoctrination in nationalities policy, and with themselves as examples firmly advance the implementation of the nationalities policy of the Chinese Communist Party. If the people as a whole do not understand this policy, then the policy cannot be translated into actual fact; furthermore, if a person serving as a Communist Party member or a revolutionary worker is blindly ignorant of the policy of the Chinese Communist Party, he certainly cannot be a good Communist Party member or a good revolutionary worker; then he definitely cannot become a really good Communist.

# Appendix A

## National Minorities in China*

| Nationalities having their own autonomous region, autonomous *chou*, or joint autonomous *chou* | Nationalities having no autonomous area, or only autonomous *hsien* | Estimated 1957 populations |
|---|---|---|
| | 1. A-ch'ang | 10,000 |
| | 2. Ch'iang | 42,000 |
| | 3. Ch'i-lao | 23,000 |
| | 4. Ching | 4,400 |
| 5. Ching-p'o | | 100,000 |
| 6. Chuang | | 7,780,000 |
| | 7. Evenki | 7,700 |
| 8. Ha-ni | | 540,000 |
| | 9. Ho-che | 600 |
| 10. Hui | | 3,930,000 |
| | 11. K'awa (Wa) | 280,000 |
| 12. Kazakh | | 530,000 |
| 13. Kirghiz | | 68,000 |

* The data in this table are derived from *Jen-min shou-ts'e 1965* (People's handbook) (Peking, 1965), pp. 108–116. Absent from this list are the names of two peoples which occur in the text: the Kao-shan and the Nung. The Kao-shan reside on Formosa and are thus beyond the reach of CCP national minority policy. The designation "Nung" is no longer in general use. It refers to a branch of the Chuang located in southeastern Yunnan; it is now included among the Chuang.

| Nationalities having their own autonomous region, autonomous *chou*, or joint autonomous *chou* | Nationalities having no autonomous area, or only autonomous *hsien* | Estimated 1957 populations |
|---|---|---|
| 14. Korean | | 1,250,000 |
| | 15. La-hu | 180,000 |
| 16. Li | | 390,000 |
| 17. Li-su | | 310,000 |
| | 18. Manchu | 2,430,000 |
| | 19. Mao-nan | 24,000 |
| | 20. Men-pa | 3,800 |
| 21. Miao | | 2,680,000 |
| | 22. Mo-lao | 44,000 |
| 23. Mongol | | 1,640,000 |
| | 24. Na-hsi | 150,000 |
| | 25. Nu | 13,000 |
| | 26. Olunch'un | 2,400 |
| 27. Pai (Min-chia) | | 680,000 |
| | 28. Pao-an | 5,500 |
| | 29. Peng-lung | 6,300 |
| 30. Pu-yi | | 1,310,000 |
| | 31. Pu-lang | 41,000 |
| | 32. P'u-mi | 15,000 |
| | 33. Russian | 9,700 |
| | 34. Salar | 31,000 |
| | 35. Shui (Shui-chia) | 160,000 |
| | 36. Sibo | 21,000 |
| | 37. Tahur | 50,000 |
| | 38. Tajik | 15,000 |
| | 39. Tatar | 4,300 |
| 40. T'ai (Thai) | | 500,000 |
| 41. Tibetan | | 2,770,000 |
| | 42. T'u (Monguor) | 63,000 |
| 43. T'u-chia | | 600,000 |
| | 44. Tu-lung | 2,700 |
| 45. T'ung | | 820,000 |
| | 46. Tung-hsiang | 150,000 |
| 47. Uighur | | 3,900,000 |
| | 48. Uzbek | 11,000 |
| | 49. Yao | 740,000 |
| 50. Yi (Lolo) | | 3,260,000 |
| | 51. Yü | 220,000 |
| | 52. Yü-ku | 4,600 |

# Appendix B

"Resolution of the First All-China Congress of Soviets on the Question of National Minorities in China"

(Adopted by the Congress at Juichin, Kiangsi, November 1931)*

1. There are many national minorities living on Chinese territory, as, for example, Mongolians, Tibetans, Mohammedans, Koreans, Annamites, Miao, Yao, and others in Sinkiang, Hunan, and Kwangsi Provinces, and the Moslems in Kansu, Szechuan, and other provinces. For a very great number of years Chinese emperors, landlords, government officials, and merchants' and usurers' capital have oppressed them and domineered over them. After the formation of the Chinese Republic, these national minorities were not only left without national emancipation, but on the contrary the yoke of exploitation of the Chinese militarists, landlords, government officials, and merchants' and usurers' capital became heavier still. Unprecedented famine and ruin devastated the areas populated by

* *Fundamental Laws of the Chinese Soviet Republic*, with an introduction by Bela Kun (New York, 1934), pp. 78–83. By permission of International Publishers Co. Inc.

the national minorities (for example Kansu and Sinkiang). Every form of resistance, every protest movement on the part of these national minorities was put down with unheard-of cruelty (for example, the punitive tactics of Feng Yü-hsiang against the Moslems).

The Kuomintang, which represents the Chinese landlords among the bourgeoisie, still further increased the oppression, exploitation, and persecution of the national minorities. All the talk about so-called "equality of nations" and a "Five Nations' Republic" is just so much deception on the part of the Kuomintang Government.

The First All-China Congress of Soviets of Workers', Peasants', and Soldiers' Deputies calls upon the Chinese workers and peasants as well as all the toiling masses of the national minorities living on the territory of China to fight resolutely against Sun Yat-sen's so-called "nationalism," since it fully satisfies the interests of the landlords and the bourgeoisie but cannot in any way or by any means be acceptable to the Chinese Soviet Republic.

2. The Chinese workers, peasants, soldiers, and all the toiling masses shall fight determinedly against the oppression of national minorities, and strive for their complete emancipation. In view of this, the First All-China Congress of Soviets of Workers', Peasants', and Soldiers' Deputies declares that the Chinese Soviet Republic categorically and unconditionally recognizes the right of national minorities to self-determination. This means that in districts like Mongolia, Tibet, Sinkiang, Yunnan, Kweichow, and others, where the majority of the population belongs to non-Chinese nationalities, the toiling masses of these nationalities shall have the right to determine for themselves whether they wish to leave the Chinese Soviet Republic and create their own independent state, or whether they wish to join the Union of Soviet Republics, or form an autonomous area inside the Chinese Soviet Republic. The Chinese Soviet Republic shall do its utmost to assist and encourage all the struggles of the national minorities against imperialism,

against the Chinese militarists, landlords, government officials, and merchants' and usurers' capital. The Chinese Soviet Republic shall also support the national-revolutionary movement and the struggle waged against the attacks and threats of the imperialists and the Kuomintang militarists by these national minorities that have already won their independence as, for example, the Outer Mongolian National Republic.

3. At the same time the First All-China Congress of Soviets of Workers', Peasants', and Soldiers' Deputies deems it necessary to point out that it is not only the toiling masses of the national minorities but also the masses of the Chinese workers and peasants themselves who suffer oppression, exploitation, and persecution at the hands of the imperialists and Chinese militarists, landlords and bourgeois. At the same time the toiling masses of the national minorities are oppressed and exploited not only by the imperialist and Chinese militarists, landlords, and the bourgeoisie but also by their own ruling classes: in Mongolia, by the princes and "Living Buddhas"; in Tibet, by the lamas; in Korea, by the gentry; while the Miao, the Yao, and other nationalities are exploited by their own *t'u-ssu* and so on. These ruling classes are the tools of the imperialists, the landlords, and the bourgeoisie, for they assist the latter in oppressing and exploiting the toiling masses of the national minorities.

Consequently the First All-China Congress of Soviets of Workers', Peasants', and Soldiers' Deputies calls upon the toiling masses of the national minorities to unite with the Chinese masses of workers and peasants in a joint struggle against their common oppressors and exploiters, against imperialism and the rule of the native landlords and bourgeoisie, and for the creation of a Workers' and Peasants' Soviet Government. At the same time the First All-China Congress of Soviets of Workers', Peasants', and Soldiers' Deputies calls upon the toiling masses of the national minorities to fight against their own oppressors, against their own ruling classes, which, behind a smokescreen of nationalist slogans, savagely denounce the Soviet Union and the Chinese Soviet Republic, for the sole reason that both these states belong to the workers and peasants and engage in irreconcilable battle against the imperialists and exploiters.

4. The First All-China Congress of Soviets of Workers', Peasants', and Soldiers' Deputies openly declares before the toiling masses of all nationalities in China that it is the purpose of the Chinese Soviet Republic to create a single state for them, without national barriers, and to uproot all national enmity and national prejudices. In order to achieve this object, the Chinese Soviet Republic shall extend the operation of all its laws — agrarian, labor, suffrage, and so on — unconditionally to all the toiling masses living on the territory of the Chinese Soviet Republic, irrespective of the nationality to which they belong.

The Chinese Soviet Republic must pay special attention to the development of the productive forces and to raising the level of culture in the backward national autonomous areas of the Chinese Soviet Republic. Schools must be opened in which the instruction shall be in the native languages of the national minorities; publishing houses must be founded, and the use of native languages, both written and oral, must be permitted in all governmental departments; the local workers and peasants from the small nationalities must form cadres for the work of state administration, and Chinese big-power chauvinism must be resolutely combated.

5. The First All-China Congress of Soviets of Workers', Peasants', and Soldiers' Deputies is of the opinion that today there is only one country in the whole world — namely, the Soviet Union — which has actually overthrown the power of its landlords and bourgeoisie once and for all, and where the worker and peasant masses have achieved complete emancipation. The Soviet Union is the only country in which there is no persecution of one nation by another, where there are no national animosities, where the national question has indeed been solved.

The First All-China Congress of Workers', Peasants', and Soldiers' Deputies holds that the yoke of international imperialism can be thrown off and oppression and exploitation be abolished only in alliance with the worker and peasant masses of the whole world, only in alliance with all oppressed nations and under the guidance of the Soviet Union.

Therefore, the First All-China Congress of Soviets of Workers', Peasants', and Soldiers' Deputies resolves:

(a) In the Fundamental Law (Constitution) of the Chinese Soviet Republic it shall be clearly stated that all national minorities within the confines of China shall have the right to national self-determination, including secession from China and the formation of independent states, and that the Chinese Soviet Republic fully and unconditionally recognizes the independence of the Outer Mongolian People's Republic.

(b) The toiling masses of all national minorities on the territory of the Chinese Soviet Republic, especially in those areas where the majority of the population is Chinese, shall enjoy absolute equality with the latter, nor shall any of their legal rights or obligations be denied or abridged on account of nationality.

(c) The Provisional Soviet Government is hereby instructed to devote special attention to the development of the productive forces in the national republics and autonomous areas that may be attached to the Chinese Soviet Republic. It shall raise their cultural level, shall train and promote local cadres so as to abolish completely all national animosities and national prejudices and create a single workers' and peasants' state without any national barriers whatsoever.

(d) The Provisional Soviet Government is hereby further instructed to take all steps necessary to render active and concrete aid and support to the national emancipation struggle of the minor nationalities against the Kuomintang militarists, against all Chinese and non-Chinese landlords and capitalists.

(e) Finally, the Provisional Soviet Government is hereby instructed immediately to establish the closest political, economical, and cultural ties with the Soviet Union.

# Appendix C

## Excerpts from the "Common Program" and the "Constitution"

*Chapter VI of the* Common Program, *entitled "Policy Toward Nationalities," reads as follows:**

ARTICLE 50. All nationalities within the boundaries of the People's Repulic of China are equal. They shall establish unity and mutual aid among themselves, and shall oppose imperialism and their own public enemies, so that the People's Republic of China will become a big fraternal and cooperative family composed of all nationalities. Great nation chauvinism shall be opposed. Acts involving discrimination, oppression, and splitting of the unity of the various nationalities shall be prohibited.

ARTICLE 51. Regional autonomy shall be exercised in areas where national minorities are concentrated, and various kinds of autonomy organizations of the different nationalities shall

* "The Common Program of the Chinese People's Political Consultative Conference [CPPCC]," in *The Important Documents of the First Plenary Session of the CPPCC* (Peking: Foreign Languages Press, 1949).

be set up according to the size of the respective populations and regions. In places where different nationalities live together and in the autonomous areas of the national minorities, the different nationalities shall each have an appropriate number of representatives in the local organs of political power.

ARTICLE 52. All national minorities within the boundaries of the People's Republic of China shall have the right to join the People's Liberation Army and to organize local people's security forces in accordance with the unified military system of the state.

ARTICLE 53. All national minorities shall have freedom to develop their dialects and languages, to preserve or reform their traditions, customs, and religious beliefs. The People's Government shall assist the masses of the people of all national minorities to develop their political, economic, cultural, and educational construction work.

*Paragraph #5 of the Preamble of the* Constitution *reads as follows:*†

All nationalities of our country are united in one great family of free and equal nations. This unity of China's nationalities will continue to gain in strength, founded as it is on ever-growing friendship and mutual aid among themselves, and on the struggle against imperialism, against public enemies of the people within the nationalities, and against both dominant-nation chauvinism and local nationalism. In the course of economic and cultural development, the state will concern itself with the needs of the different nationalities, and, in the matter of socialist transformation, pay full attention to the special characteristics in the development of each.

† This and the following passage are from the "Constitution of the People's Republic of China [CPR]," in *Documents of the First Session of the First National People's Congress of the CPR* (Peking: Foreign Languages Press, 1955).

*Article #3 of Chapter I, "General Principles," of the* Constitution *reads as follows:*

The People's Republic of China is a unified, multinational state.

All the nationalities are equal. Discrimination against, or oppression of, any nationality and acts that undermine the unity of the nationalities are prohibited.

All the nationalities have freedom to use and foster the growth of their spoken and written languages, and to preserve or reform their own customs or ways.

Regional autonomy applies in areas entirely or largely inhabited by national minorities. National autonomous areas are inalienable parts of the People's Republic of China.

*Section V (Articles 67-72), "The Organs of Self-Government of National Autonomous Areas," in Chapter II of the* Constitution *provides an outline of the structure of national regional autonomy. This section is not reproduced here, however, since it reveals little if anything about the real locus of authority in national minority areas.*

# Appendix D

## Party and State Organizations Concerned with National Minority Affairs*

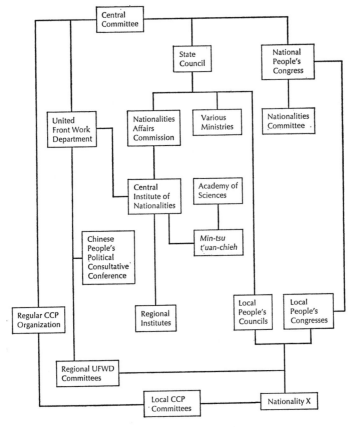

* Based on author's conjecture.

# Bibliographical Guide to the National Minority Policy of the Chinese Communist Party

## A. BASIC DOCUMENTS

National minority policy is an element in the matrix of Chinese Communist policy which expresses a constantly evolving synthesis of ideology and reality, of Marxist-Leninist theory and the actual situation in China at any given time. This synthesis is periodically elaborated by the CCP at its national Congresses as well as at the intervening plenums of the Central Committee. Pronouncements by Mao Tse-tung and Liu Shaoch'i, together with a few state documents, have a similar status. My own search has shown the following items to be the most significant documents on the CCP's national minority policy. The periodization is my own, and is tentative.

### 1. *Self-determination phase*

"Manifesto of the Second National Congress of the CCP" (July 1922), résumé in BS&F (Conrad Brandt, Benjamin Schwartz, and John K. Fairbank, *A Documentary History of Chinese Communism* [Cambridge, Massachusetts, 1952]), especially p. 64.

"Political Resolution of the Sixth National Congress of the CCP" (September 1928), in BS&F, especially p. 132.

"Constitution of the Soviet Republic" (November 1931), in BS&F, especially p. 223.

"Resolution of the First All-China Congress of Soviets on the

Question of National Minorities in China" (November 1931),
Appendix B of the present work.

## 2. *Anti-imperialist phase*

"Report of the President of the Central Executive Committee
of the Chinese Soviet Republic, Mao Tse-tung" (January 1934),
in Victor A. Yakhontoff, *The Chinese Soviets* (New York,
1934), especially pp. 276–277.

Mao Tse-tung, "On Japanese Imperialism," in Edgar Snow,
"Interviews with Mao Tse-tung" in *China: The March Toward
Unity*, edited by Workers Library Publishers (New York,
1937), pp. 33–50, especially p. 40.

"The Ten Great Policies of the CCP for Anti-Japanese Resistance and National Salvation" (August 1937), in BS&F, especially p. 243.

"Sixth Plenum of the Sixth CCP Central Committee"
(November 1938), summarized by Hsieh Ho-ch'ou in *Min-tsu
t'uan-chieh*, No. 1 (1960), pp. 3–6. Hsieh's article is discussed
in *China News Analysis* (Hong Kong), No. 431 (3 August
1962).

Mao Tse-tung (and others), *The Chinese Revolution and the
Chinese Communist Party* (December 1939) (Peking: Foreign
Languages Press, 1954), especially pp. 2–4.

## 3. *Regional-autonomy phase*

Mao Tse-tung, "On Coalition Government" (April 1945);
report to the Seventh National Congress of the CCP. In BS&F,
pp. 295–318, Section 9, "The Problem of National Minorities."

"The Common Program of the Chinese People's Political
Consultative Conference" (September 1949); see Appendix C
of the present work.

"General Program of the People's Republic of China for
the Implementation of Regional Autonomy for Nationalities"
(August 1952), in *Policy Toward Nationalities* (Peking: Foreign Languages Press, 1953), pp. 1–13.

Liu Shao-ch'i, "Report on the Draft Constitution of the People's Republic of China," in *Documents of the First Session of the First National People's Congress of the People's Republic of China* (Peking: Foreign Languages Press, 1955), pp. 9–73, especially Section 4, "The Question of National Regional Autonomy."

"Constitution of the People's Republic of China" (September 1954); see Appendix C of the present work.

### 4. *Socialist-transformation stage*

Liu Shao-ch'i, "Political Report of the Central Committee to the Eighth National Congress of the CCP" (September 1956), in Bowie and Fairbank (*Communist China, 1955–1959: Policy Documents with Analysis*, with a foreword by Robert R. Bowie and John K. Fairbank [Cambridge, Massachusetts, 1962]), Document No. 9, Section 4, "The Political Life of the State."

Mao Tse-tung, "On the Correct Handling of Contradictions among the People" (February 1957), in Bowie and Fairbank, Document No. 14, Section 6, "The Question of National Minorities."

Teng Hsiao-p'ing (General Secretary of the CCP Central Committee), "Report on the Rectification Campaign" to the Third Plenum of the Eighth Central Committee (September 1957), in Bowie and Fairbank, Document No. 19, Section 5, "On Minority Nationalities."

Wang Feng (Vice-Chairman of the Nationalities Affairs Commission), "The Great Victory in Our Nationalities Policy" (September 1959), in Bowie and Fairbank, Document No. 44, Section 6, "The Question of National Minorities."

Ulanfu (Central Committee member and Chairman of the Inner Mongolia Autonomous Region government), "Ceaselessly Develop the Great Unity among All the Nationalities of China," *Hung ch'i* (Red flag), No. 19 (1959), pp. 43–50 (translated in U.S. Consulate General, Hong Kong, *Selections from China Mainland Magazines* [SCMM], No. 189).

5. *Current phase*

"In National Minority Areas Positively Implement the Spirit of the Party's Tenth Plenum, Further Strengthen the Collective Economy of the People's Communes, and Expand Agricultural and Pastoral Production," *Min-tsu t'uan-chieh,* No. 11 (1962), editorial, pp. 2–6 (translated in SCMM, No. 347).

Liu Ch'un (Vice-Chairman of the Nationality Affairs Commission), "Class Struggle and the National Question in Our Country at the Present Time," *Hung ch'i* No. 12 (1964), pp. 16–25 (translated in SCMM, No. 428).

## B. *NATIONALITIES JOURNALS*

The chief Chinese Communist publication on national minority affairs is *Min-tsu t'uan-chieh* (Nationalities unity), a monthly journal which has appeared continuously since 1959. Like its predecessors, *Min-tsu t'uan-chieh* is published by the Nationalities Institute of the Chinese Academy of Sciences. It took the place of *Min-tsu yen-chiu* (Nationalities research), which had enjoyed a life span of only a year after having displaced an earlier journal, *Min-tsu wen-t'i i-tsung* (Translations on nationalities problems), in September 1958. *Min-tsu wen-t'i i-tsung* had been appearing since 1954 (see Introduction, p. xvi). The Library of Congress and Harvard University each possess a few issues (not the same ones) of *Min-tsu wen-t'i i-tsung,* which I myself have not used. The Library of Congress has a complete collection (1958, nos. 1–4; 1959, nos. 1–9) and Harvard a partial collection (lacking the issues for 1958) of *Min-tsu yen-chiu,* which was a scholarly journal of some distinction prior to its demise in September 1958 (the editorial board had already confessed its "errors" in February). Most issues of *Min-tsu t'uan-chieh* are available in the Library of Congress, Harvard University, and the British Museum. While less academic than *Min-tsu yen-chiu, Min-tsu t'uan-chieh* is a serious journal that serves the double purpose of interpreting CCP national minority policy and of studying the socioeconomic changes in the lives of China's non-Han peoples as a result of their "transformation." Many of the more important articles from *Min-tsu t'uan-chieh* have appeared in translation in U.S. Consulate General, Hong Kong, *Selections from China Mainland Magazines* and in U.S. Department of Commerce, Joint Publications Research Service *Reports*. On a more propagandistic level is the monthly *Min-tsu hua-pao* (Nationalities pictorial), which is published in eighteen languages and has a wide international distribution.

## C. *BOOKS AND ARTICLES*

Chang Hsia-min, *Kung-fei pao-cheng hsia chih pien-chiang min-tsu* (The border peoples under the tyranny of the Communist bandits) (Taipei, 1958). Castigates CCP nationalities policy as but a cheap imitation of Soviet policy, the effect of which is to divide rather than to unite the various peoples of China; provides valuable factual material.

Basil Davidson, "China's non-Chinese Peoples," *The Listener* (London) (17 January 1957). A sympathetic appraisal by an Englishman who has visited Communist China and written a book on Sinkiang province.

John DeFrancis, "National and Minority Policies," *The Annals of the American Academy of Political and Social Science*, Vol. 277 (September 1951): *Report on China*, pp. 146–155. Dated though it is, this is still the best study of Chinese Communist national minority policy: the author makes good use of Chinese materials and successfully projects the psychological milieu in which the CCP has grappled with the nationalities problem.

"The Existing National Autonomy Areas in China," in U.S. Consulate General, Hong Kong, *Current Background*, No. 430 (10 December 1956). Provides a translation of data on forty-five national minorities as published in *Shih-shih shou-ts'e* (Current affairs handbook), No. 17 (10 September 1956). Like other U.S. government translations, this material is valuable not only because it provides pertinent information in English, but also because the original Chinese material is relatively inaccessible and often simply unobtainable.

Fei Hsiao-t'ung, "Free and Equal Family," *People's China* (16 May 1955), pp. 16–20. A piece of ordinary propaganda to which Fei put his name; reviews constitutional provisions pertaining to minorities and the great accomplishments in the frontier regions since Liberation.

Fei Hsiao-t'ung and others, *Shen-ma shih min-tsu ch'ü-yü tzu-chih* (What is national regional autonomy?) (Hong Kong, 1956). This book is of interest less for its content, which is rather meager, than for the fact that it was edited by Professor Fei, who has been a *cause célèbre* of Western-trained sociologists in China.

Fei Hsiao-t'ung and Lin Yüeh-hua, a series of articles in *Jen-min jih-pao* (translated in *Current Background,* No. 430): "A Study of the Question of 'Different Nationalities' among the Minority Nationalities of China" (10 August 1956); "A Study of the Social Nature of the Minority Nationalities" (14 August 1956); "A Study of the Culture and Life of the Minority Nationalities" (16 August 1956). The purpose of these articles was in large part polemical, as described in my introduction.

Stanley Ghosh, *Embers in Cathay* (Garden City, New York, 1961). A journalistic survey of China's minorities under the "cruel regime of Red China" written by a Bengali who lives in the United States.

"Guide to Minority Nationalities and Autonomous Areas of Communist China," in U.S. Department of Commerce, Joint Publications Research Service (JPRS), *Report* No. 19,670 (12 June 1963): *Communist China Digest,* No. 93, pp. 1–44. A useful compendium gathered from a wide range of Chinese Communist publications.

Gutorm Gjessing, "Chinese Anthropology and New China's Policy Towards Her Minorities," *Acta Sociologica* (Copenhagen), Vol. 2 (1957), pp. 45–68. A penetrating analysis by a

Swedish sociologist who visited Peking, and the Nationalities Institute there, in 1954.

(Mrs.) Elsie Hawtin, "The 'Hundred Flowers Movement' and the Role of the Intellectual in China. Fei Hsiao-t'ung: A Case History," *Papers on China* (Harvard University, Center for East Asian Studies), Vol. 12 (December 1958), pp. 147–198. Although Mrs. Hawtin is not especially interested in national minority policy, her thorough treatment of Professor Fei's personal crisis is of great value.

Harold C. Hinton, "The National Minorities in China," *Far Eastern Economic Review*, Vol. 19 (1955): Part I in No. 11 (September 15), pp. 321–325; Part II in No. 12 (September 22), pp. 367–372. Harshly critical of the CCP's policy of regional autonomy.

G. F. Hudson, "The Nationalities of China," *St. Antony's Papers*, Vol. 7 (London, 1960), pp. 51–61. An essay on the distribution and historical role of China's non-Han peoples, and on CCP national minority policy in the 1950's. This study makes valuable comparisons between Soviet and Chinese Communist policies.

*Jen-min shou-ts'e* (People's handbook). Published annually in several Chinese cities by *Ta kung pao*; contains data (generally scanty) on the national minorities.

P. H. M. Jones, numerous articles in the *Far Eastern Economic Review* (Hong Kong). Studies of individual minorities and regions have not been included in this bibliography since they do not relate directly to the general question of the CCP's national minority policy. Because of the range of his research on the situation of China's non-Han peoples, however, exception must be made for Mr. Jones' articles, which provide a fairly comprehensive survey of CCP policy in national minority regions. Between 1960 and 1964 alone, he produced nearly twenty important articles bearing on this problem.

B. F. Kasatkin, "Solution of the National Question in the Chinese People's Republic," *Sovetskoye Vostokovedeniye*

(Moscow), No. 4 (1956), pp. 16–27. Uncritically describes and praises CCP policy.

K. F. Kotov, *Autonomy of Local Nationalities in the Chinese People's Republic* (Moscow, 1959), translated in JPRS, *Report No. 3547* (18 July 1960). Only Sinkiang province is treated in detail in this thorough but uncritical study of CCP policy.

Lin Yüeh-hua, "Problems Confronting Chinese Ethnographers in Connection with Solving the Nationalities Question in the Chinese People's Republic," *Sovetskaya Etnografia*, No. 3 (1956), pp. 79–91, translated in JPRS, *Report No. 16,431*. In this professional address delivered in Leningrad, Professor Lin discusses some of the real problems encountered in translating CCP ideology on the national question into practice.

Lin Yü-lüeh, *Chung-kung tsen-yang tui-tai shao-shu min-tsu?* (How do the Chinese Communists treat the national minorities?) (Hong Kong, 1953). A brief, general survey in the form of questions and answers. It is addressed mainly to overseas Chinese.

Roderick MacFarquhar, "The Minorities," *New Leader*, Vol. 42, No. 23 (8 June 1959), pp. 17–21. One of a series of articles on "Communist China's First Decade."

"Les Minorités ethniques de la Chine continentale," *Notes et Etudes documentaires* (Paris), No. 2639 (27 February 1960). An extensive and competent survey.

*Min-tsu cheng-ts'e wen-hsien wei-pien* (Collected documents on nationalities policy) (Peking, 1953), covering the years 1949 to 1952; another volume with the same title, with documents pertaining to the years 1954 to 1957, was published in Peking in 1958. These documents comprise detailed measures passed by the State Council, progress reports on the implementation of policy in different regions of the country, editorials from *Jen-min jih-pao*, etc. The earlier volume is the more valuable.

George Moseley, "China's Fresh Approach to the National Minority Question," *China Quarterly* (London), No. 24 (September–December 1965), pp. 15–27. A review of trends since 1962.

"National Minorities," *China News Analysis* (Hong Kong), No. 431 (3 August 1962). This perceptive appraisal is but one of a number of reports dealing more or less directly with the national minorities which have appeared in the weekly, *China News Analysis*.

George N. Patterson, "Treatment of Minorities," in Werner Klatt (editor), *The Chinese Model* (Hong Kong, 1965), pp. 154–168. A critical survey of CCP policy in Tibet and other frontier regions.

*Policy Towards Nationalities of the Chinese People's Republic* (Peking: Foreign Languages Press, 1953). Contains important documents as well as propaganda.

T. R. Rakhimov, "Successful Solution of the Nationality Problem in the Chinese People's Republic," *Problemy Vostokovedeniya*, No. 4 (Moscow, 1959), pp. 36–47. A serious appraisal that takes into account the historical evolution of CCP policy and the Marxist-Leninist theoretical position that must be adapted to Chinese conditions.

Nicholas Read-Collins, "Peking and the Minority Problem," *Eastern World* (London), Vol. 7, No. 3 (March 1953), pp. 19–22. A sympathetic account; the author visited the Nationalities Institute in Peking.

Subhash Chandra Sarker, "China's Policy Towards Minorities," *World Today* (London), Vol. 15, No. 10 (October 1959), pp. 408–416. A rather superficial summary.

Henry G. Schwartz, "Communist Language Policies for China's Ethnic Minorities: The First Decade," *China Quarterly* (London), No. 12 (October–December 1962), pp. 170–182. Argues that language policy is but an aspect of Peking's attempt to absorb the national minorities in Han culture.

Sakamoto Koretada, "Chūgoku no shōsū minzoku mondai" (China's national minority question), in Ajiya seigaku kai (Asia politics and economics association), *Gendai Chūgoku no kadai* (Problems of contemporary China) (Tokyo, 1964), pp. 172–200. A brilliant discussion of the national minority policy of the CCP; covers historical background and theoretical basis as well as current policy.

"Shōsū minzoku seisaku" (National minority policy), in *Chūgoku nenkan* (China yearbook) (Tokyo, 1955), pp. 174–180. A general survey, based on the available Chinese Communist sources, with special sections on a few of the major national minority regions. There is a similar entry in the *Shin Chūgoku nenkan* (New China yearbook) (Tokyo, 1962).

G. A. von Stackelberg, "The Chinese Communist Party's Nationality Policy," *Bulletin of the Institute for the Study of the History and Culture of the USSR* (Munich), Vol. 1, No. 5 (August 1954). A superficial piece based on a hostile interpretation of Soviet sources.

Edgar Tomson, *Die Volksrepublik China und das Recht nationaler Minderheiten* (Frankfurt am Main, 1963). An extensive survey of the relevant documents, with a valuable bibliography.

Tsung Yun, "China's National Minorities," *People's China* (Peking), No. 11 (1954), pp. 17–23. Provides basic information on the national minorities.

U.S. Department of Commerce, *China: Provisional Atlas of Communist Administrative Units* (Washington, D. C., 1959). Shows boundaries of national autonomous areas.

Wang Shu-tang, *China: Land of Many Nationalities* (Peking: Foreign Languages Press, 1955). A propagandistic review.

# Index